TRANSFORMING PROBLEMS INTO HAPPINESS

TRANSFORMING

PROBLEMS

into HAPPINESS

Lama Zopa Rinpoche

Foreword by His Holiness the Dalai Lama

WISDOM PUBLICATIONS • BOSTON

Wisdom Publications
199 Elm Street
Somerville, Massachusetts 02144 USA

Tulku Thondup's translation of *Instructions on Turning Happiness and Suffering into the Path of Enlightenment* is excerpted from *Enlightened Living: Teachings of Tibetan Buddhist Matsters,* courtesy of Ranjung Yeshe Publications, Kathmandu, Nepal.

Library of Congress Cataloging-in-Publication Data
Thubten Zopa, Rinpoche, 1946-
    Transforming problems into happiness / Lama Zopa Rinpoche ; foreword by His Holiness the Dalai Lama.
        p.   cm.
    ISBN 0861711947 (alk. paper)
    Includes the translation of the original text.
    Includes bibliographical references.
    1. 'Jig-med-bstan-pa'i-ñi-ma, Rdo Grub-chen III, 1865?-1926. Rdo Grub-bstan-pa'i-ñi-ma'i skyid sdug lam khyer. 2. Spiritual life—Buddhism
BQ5660.T48 2001   2001-022242

ISBN 0-86171-194-7

06 05 04 03 02
6   5   4   3   2

Cover images: clouds © Photodisc and fire © Digital Vision
Design by Gopa and the Bear

Wisdom Publications' books are printed on acid-free paper and meet the guidelines for permanence and durability of the Committee on Production Guidelines for Book Longevity of the Council on Library Resources.

Printed in Canada.

Contents

Publisher's Acknowledgment

The Publisher gratefully acknowledges the generous help of the Hershey Family Foundation in sponsoring the publication of this book.

Foreword by His Holiness the Dalai Lama

I BELIEVE THAT THE PURPOSE of our lives is to achieve happiness. But happiness is of two kinds: one that derives from physical comfort and the other which essentially flows from our minds and our thoughts. Of these two, the happiness that derives from the mind is the more important. If our mind is calm and happy, we can put up with physical discomfort, but sensual pleasure alone will never set the mind at ease. When our minds are restless and disturbed, no matter how much luxury or physical comfort we may enjoy, these things alone will not make us happy.

The importance of our mental experience gives rise to the question, "Can we train the mind?" The Buddha explained many methods and paths by which we can purify our minds and achieve the fully awakened state of buddhahood. Among these, there is a special instruction called mind training. This instruction outlines the very heart of the Buddhist practice, cultivation of the awakening mind. These simple but far-reaching techniques for training the mind, particularly those that deal with concern for others and turning adversity to advantage, have virtually become part of the Tibetan character. It is this latter technique that Zopa Rinpoche particularly deals with in this book. And it is this pattern of thought, transforming problems into happiness, that has enabled the Tibetan people to maintain their dignity and spirit in the face of great difficulties. Indeed I have found this advice of great practical benefit in my own life.

Zopa Rinpoche has immersed himself in both the study and practice of the mind-training tradition, and in his travels around the world he is constantly meeting people who wish for happiness, but instead are beset by problems. He draws on a wealth of experience. Here he has taken as the primary focus of his advice a short text by the great scholar and remarkable yogi, Dodrupchen Jigme Tenpe Nyima. So, the source of the teaching is impeccable; what remains is for readers to put what they read into practice. I have no doubt that those who do will, over a period of time, notice a change in their mental attitudes and responses to people and events. Their minds will become more disciplined and positive. And I am sure they will find their own sense of happiness grow as they contribute to the greater happiness of others. I offer my prayers that readers of this new edition who make this their goal will be blessed with success.

The Dalai Lama
February 14, 2001

1

The Purpose of Life

You have this

precious human body

in order to serve

other living beings.

This precious human body

THE PURPOSE OF HAVING this precious human body is not simply to achieve happiness for oneself, but to eliminate the suffering of all other beings and to bring them happiness as well. This is the purpose of each of our lives. This human body is precious because with it you have the capacity and opportunity to pursue spiritual development in order to serve other living beings.

Everyone wants happiness; no one wants suffering. The happiness we need is not just ordinary, fleeting happiness; what we really need is ultimate happiness, the unsurpassed, unshakable happiness of enlightenment. When people go shopping, for example, they want the things that are the best, that will last the longest; in the same way, everyone wants the longest-lasting, highest happiness. According to their understanding of what level of happiness is achievable, everyone attempts to obtain whatever is, in their view, the highest happiness.

The Buddha's teachings, called the Dharma, tell us the highest happiness achievable is enlightenment. The only reason anyone would not want to achieve enlightenment is that they lack Dharma wisdom. Lacking Dharma wisdom means simply being unaware that there exists a happiness higher than ordinary happiness. Anyone who has encountered the Dharma and studied it sincerely knows that one can be liberated from the bondage of suffering and can experience peerless happiness, that one can put an end to all obscurations, and that one can attain all the realizations of a buddha. Of course a person who knows these things can be achieved wants to achieve them.

With such an understanding, it becomes clear that the greatest benefit anyone can offer living beings is to lead them to the enlightened state. In order to reach this, you have to follow a path that actually leads to enlightenment. Therefore, you have to know all the various methods, without the slightest mistake. In order to do this, you must first achieve enlightenment yourself. By achieving enlightenment, you achieve the state of omniscient mind of a buddha. To be most effective in revealing the path to others, you need to be able to see fully and exactly every single characteristic of their minds. For, as living beings have various characteristics and levels of intelligence, a variety of methods are needed to guide them. Only the omniscient mind of a buddha knows every single characteristic and level of intelligence of living beings and all the methods needed to liberate them.

Mahayana thought transformation

In order to achieve omniscient mind, you need to follow the path to omniscient mind. You need to practice the entire graduated path to enlightenment, what is called in Tibetan the *lamrim*. This graduated path contains the essence of the entire Dharma, of all the Buddha's teachings. It is said that we are in "the quarreling age," an extremely difficult time on this earth when violence and greed are everywhere, and there are many obstacles to practicing Dharma. Even having encountered the Dharma, you will still find it extremely difficult to continue and succeed in your practice—inner and outer obstacles will pour down like rain.

In order to succeed in listening to, reflecting on, and meditating on the graduated path to enlightenment for the benefit and happiness of all sentient beings, you must learn to practice Mahayana thought transformation—and this is what this book will teach you. In Mahayana thought transformation, also called "mind training," you use whatever problems you experience to generate the realizations along the path to enlightenment within your mind. Instead of disturbing you, problems can actually help you develop your mind and even further your progress on the path to enlightenment. Without practicing thought transformation, you will be unable to complete your Dharma practice, your inner mental development. This is why I thought to explain to you a short text by Dodrupchen Rinpoche, *Instructions on Turning Happiness and Suffering into the Path of Enlightenment*.

There are various lamrim meditations that can be applied when you have problems. Dodrupchen Rinpoche's text is based on two famous texts by early Indian masters: *The Precious Garland* by Nagarjuna and *Guide to the Bodhisattva's Way of Life* by Shantideva. Dodrupchen Rinpoche, Jigme Tenpe Nyima, a highly attained lama of the Nyingma school of Tibetan Buddhism, whose holy mind had reached very high realizations of tantra, was also learned in the teachings of the great Gelug-school founder, Lama Tsongkhapa. Jigme Tenpe Nyima's teaching does not contain anything that is not also contained in such well-known texts as *The Seven-Point Mind Training* by Geshe Chekawa and *The Eight Verses* by Langri Tangpa, or in the various other teachings on thought transformation, but the way he relates the practice of lamrim to the experience of problems and obstacles is different.

With regard to this particular practice of thought transformation, there are two aspects: using suffering in the path to enlightenment and using happiness in the path to enlightenment. Here, I will be talking about how to use suffering, or problems, in the path to enlightenment and unsurpassed happiness.

2

Developing a Different Attitude to Problems

The thought of liking problems

should arise naturally,

like the thought of liking ice cream

or the thought of liking music.

IN THIS CHALLENGING MODERN TIME with many problems and much unhappiness, human beings are especially overwhelmed by suffering, and their minds are not resilient. This is because they are unable to recognize as beneficial the problems and harm they experience and to see these problems as causes of happiness. Human beings who have not encountered the Dharma are unable to recognize this and unable to train their minds in this recognition.

Instead of seeing all the problems you experience—whether caused by living beings or by situations and circumstances—as problems, you need to develop the habit of recognizing them all as beneficial conditions supporting happiness, and in fact being causes for happiness. But you can't change your perception all at once. You must begin by trying to recognize small problems as beneficial, then gradually, as you become more accustomed to this, you can start to recognize larger, more serious problems as good, even pleasurable, and ultimately necessary for your happiness. You will see everything that disturbs you as essential for achieving happiness.

But make no mistake: The practice of thought transformation is not intended to eliminate problems but rather to enable you to use the problems you experience to train your mind to move step by step along the path to enlightenment and ultimate happiness. It is not that you will no longer receive harm from other people, or from circumstances, or from disease and old age; you will simply not be disturbed by anything that happens. The events that the untrained mind perceives as problems cannot in and of themselves disturb your practice of Dharma; they cannot prevent your attainment of the realizations of the path to enlightenment. In fact, when you practice thought transformation, not only do problems not disturb you, they actually help you to develop your mind and continue your Dharma practice.

How do you use problems in support of your Dharma practice, and your attainment of happiness? You have to train your mind in two ways. First, you stop the thought of complete aversion to suffering, and second, you generate the thought of welcoming problems. When you have accomplished this and actually feel happy rather than unhappy to have problems, problems no longer become obstacles to generating the path to enlightenment within your mind.

The fault of seeing only problems

We all come to harm from other beings, from illness, and from other events and circumstances. As long as our mind is conditioned to identify such experiences as problems, we will only find more and more people and conditions disturbing. The smallest, most insignificant matter will cause great pain in our mind, and we will become upset very quickly. The root of the problem, the true cause of our suffering, is not the external being or event that brings us harm, but rather it is our strongly selfish mind.

When we habitually identify everything as a problem, even something so small as being given food that is a little cold causes great discomfort in our mind. Something a little off with the way someone dresses or looks, something not quite in line with our own idea of how it should be, becomes the cause of great suffering. If we hear a noise during the night that wakes us up, we become incredibly angry. The whole of the next day we complain about it: "Oh, I didn't get any sleep last night!" Not getting enough sleep becomes an unbelievable problem, an unbelievable suffering.

If a tiny, insignificant being, such as a flea, runs over our leg and bites us while we are sleeping or meditating, it becomes an unbelievably huge problem. Some Westerners spend thousands of dollars to go to Kathmandu, but after spending just one night there, they decide they cannot stand the uncomfortable conditions and fly back home the next day.

It is the nature of the mind to become addicted to certain ways of seeing things. By habitually seeing as a problem every tiny thing that does not accord exactly with our self-cherishing wishes, we exaggerate small things into huge problems. If we see even small sufferings as big problems and get irritated by them, we become unceasingly overwhelmed by a heavy, unhappy mind. It then becomes extremely difficult for us to bear any problem whatsoever. Everything appears threatening. Everything appears unsatisfying. Everything we hear, see, taste, smell, or touch makes us unhappy. Our mind exaggerates problems, and we find that our life is filled with irritation, depression, paranoia, and perhaps even nervous breakdowns. We are constantly overwhelmed by our completely unhappy mind, and it is very hard for us to be happy for one day, for even one hour.

We have no opportunity to experience happiness if there is nothing that we like, nothing that is satisfactory. Whatever we try, wherever we go, everything makes us unhappy.

Not realizing that this is our own doing, that we have trained our mind to this negative way of thinking, we point to external things—other beings or circumstances—as the source of our problems. The more we think that our problems come from outside, the more our anger arises. Like a fire blazing as we pour more and more oil on it, our anger blazes higher and higher, bringing greater negative karma; then unbearably great anger arises, bringing even heavier negative karma. We become angry at everything that appears to our senses, everyone and everything we see. This state is known in the Buddhist teachings as "all appearances arising as the enemy."

What is the alternative to this state? The great eleventh-century meditator Milarepa is normally pictured keeping his right hand at his ear in a gesture of listening. This is because everything appeared to Milarepa in the form of advice; everything appeared as a teaching. For skillful meditators with well-trained minds, instead of all appearances arising as the enemy, they actually appear as the opposite: as a friend and a teacher. Instead of disturbing us, everything appears as beneficial and supportive. To skillful meditators, everything appears as bliss, everything appears as a manifestation of emptiness—the ultimate nature of all things—and so, skillful meditators are unhindered by problems.

Seeing the benefits of problems

When you perceive a problem, if you remember the benefits of having problems and approach it with the practice of Mahayana thought transformation, your problem becomes desirable. Instead of hindering you, your problems become good and useful.

No matter how many problems you have, there is no point at all in being disturbed or irritated by them. When you meet miserable, undesirable conditions, it is extremely important to think over and over again of the great shortcomings of perceiving them as problems and of being irritated by them. There is no benefit perceiving circumstances in this way. It is simply unnecessary to see them as problems.

You may have a measure of control over certain situations, but there are others you just have to endure. For example, no matter how upset you are that your house is not made of gold, you have no power to turn the bricks into gold. And no matter how upset you are that the sky is not the earth, you cannot turn the sky into the earth. There is no point in expending even a moment's concern about such things. No matter how much you worry about any external problem and no matter how irritated you become, your irritation cannot make the problem go away.

As the Indian master Shantideva explains in his *Guide to the Bodhisattva's Way of Life*, if a problem can be solved, there is no point in being upset about it; there is no reason to be angry, and no reason to be depressed. And if the problem is something that cannot be changed, there is also no point in being unhappy, in disliking it, or in becoming angry. Therefore, no matter what happens, there is no point in being angry or depressed.

No matter what happens, there is always a reason to think: "This is a favorable, beneficial condition." For example, when someone is bitten by a poisonous snake, cutting away the flesh around the bite is regarded as beneficial, although it is painful. It is not considered harmful, because it protects one's life. According to the Tibetan system of medicine, when a disease contaminating the inside of your body shows some sign of coming out, it generally means that you are getting better. Its coming out of the body—instead of staying inside, getting larger and larger, and lasting a long time—is regarded as a good thing. It is still a sickness, but it is nonetheless regarded as good.

Identifying the harms you receive as problems has great shortcomings. Think of all the problems you have experienced in your life. Then contemplate over and over again the result of seeing them as problems. Has it benefited you or not? Try to see as clearly as possible the shortcomings of this attitude. Then generate a very strong positive motivation, determining that, "From now on, no matter what problems I have to face, I won't become irritated by them. I won't identify any circumstances or obstacles I experience as problems. I'll regard them as positive." Generating this brave, determined attitude is extremely important for your thought-transformation practice to succeed.

With this strong motivation as a foundation, proceed to train your mind until you become like an experienced horseman—even though his mind may be distracted, he is able to manage the horse effortlessly, no matter what it does, without falling off or endangering his life. He is able to cope because his body responds naturally to the way the horse runs. Similarly, when meeting miserable conditions or obstacles, an experienced thought-transformation practitioner immediately and effortlessly recognizes them as good. The thought of liking the problem arises naturally, like the thought of liking ice cream or the thought of liking music. When a person who enjoys music hears music, the thought of liking it arises naturally, without any need to consider the reasons.

When you meet undesirable conditions, if you spontaneously recognize them as good, you will be happy. During times of criticism, poverty, difficulties, failure, sickness, or even imminent death, nothing will disturb your mind. You will be consistently happy. Effortlessly, naturally, you will recognize the benefits of problems. And the more you see the benefits, the happier you will be to experience difficulties in your life.

By training your mind and becoming accustomed to not seeing problems as problems, even great problems of the mind and body become so easy to bear that you experience no difficulty when you encounter them. Problems become enjoyable, as light and soft as cotton.

Seeing problems as joyful

It is essential to be well prepared before actually meeting miserable conditions, since being able to use them as a basis for virtue and happiness is extremely difficult. With prior training, however, you can more easily apply the thought-transformation practice you have been practicing.

To transform problems into happiness, it is not sufficient simply to see that problems *help* your practice of virtue. This alone is not enough. You must clearly recognize that your problems are actually *necessary* conditions for your practice of virtue, and you can derive continual, stable happiness from this.

During difficult times, remember that your problems are benefiting you immensely by allowing you to achieve not only temporal happiness but also happiness in future lives, as well as liberation, and the ultimate happiness of enlightenment. Even though your problems may be very heavy and difficult to bear, remember that they are the most joyful things to have because they benefit you continuously.

As long as you see something as a problem and allow it to irritate you, you cause that problem to disturb your mind. While this is happening, there is no way to transform that suffering into Dharma practice. But when you are able to stop seeing problems as problems, you are able to use suffering in your Dharma practice. Problems actually enable you to increase your good karma. They become the cause of happiness.

It is not enough to hear me say these things; this has to come from your own experience. Of course, you cannot suddenly face big problems and transform them into the Buddhist path. As much as you are able, train your mind to transform small sufferings; then, when you experience big problems or great disasters—even death, the most fearful thing of all—you will be able to infuse them with virtue and use them in your Dharma practice to move further along the path to ultimate happiness.

Stopping the thought of disliking problems and generating the thought of liking them makes the mind happy. With this attitude, you can always maintain your practice without depression or discouragement. Because you have cultivated a strong belief that experiencing problems is desirable and joyful, even though you may have a problem, it will not disturb your mind and you will easily be able to bear it.

This is how you can utilize disease and other problems in your life, such as adversaries you believe are disturbing your happiness or your Dharma practice. Even if they persist in what they are doing, they will be utterly unable to interfere with your happiness and so cannot disturb your mind.

In short, train your mind to see the beauty in all problems. In order for problems to appear desirable to you, you have to stop looking at the shortcomings of situations. Put all your effort into looking at the benefits of problems. Whether a life situation is wonderful or not depends on the way your mind perceives and interprets it. You can choose to label an experience "wonderful" or "problematic." It depends completely upon your mind, upon your interpretation. Your experiences will definitely change as you change the way you think.

When I was in Lawudo Cave many years ago, I found a text called *Opening the Door of Dharma: The Initial Stage of Training the Mind in the Graduated Path to Enlightenment*. This was the only general text I found there, among the many other handwritten manuscripts of initiations and deity practices. I must have read a lot in that text about the shortcomings of grasping onto worldly things, such as material goods or fame. After that, when the local people brought me offerings—for example, a plate filled with corn and rice with some money on top, which according to their custom is called a mandala—I was very fearful because I realized the dangers of those offerings; I was afraid of receiving a reputation and becoming famous. There was much fear in my heart because I saw the pitfalls so clearly. So you see, at that time I was trying to practice Dharma. Now, however, I have sunk completely into the quagmire of worldly concern!

3

Happiness and Suffering
Are Created by Your Mind

Happiness and suffering

are dependent upon your mind,

upon your interpretation.

They do not come from outside,

from others.

All of your happiness

and all of your suffering

are created by you,

by your own mind.

The tip of the wish

BUDDHIST TEACHINGS TELL US, "All of existence depends on the tip of the wish." All happiness and all suffering depend on our wish, our motivation. The most oppressive suffering of the hell realms and the highest happiness of the state of omniscient mind come from the mind.

With few exceptions, all actions we perform with our body, speech, and mind out of worldly concern—concern only for our own happiness in this life alone—are nonvirtuous and thus result in suffering.

All actions of body, speech, and mind done with the wish that seeks happiness beyond this life, seeks the happiness of future lives, or seeks the happiness of all beings, are virtuous and cause our happiness. Through these actions, we can experience happiness in future lives, as well as in this life. All actions of body, speech, and mind done with the wish to achieve liberation from the bondage of karma and disturbing thoughts are virtuous and are themselves the cause of liberation. And all actions of body, speech, and mind done with the wish to achieve enlightenment for the sake of all beings are not only virtuous but are also the cause of enlightenment. Once you realize this, you perform positive actions all day and night, and all these actions become the cause to achieve the ultimate and peerless happiness of the state of enlightenment.

This is why the Buddha's teachings say that all of existence depends on the tip of a wish. Everything depends completely on the mind. Temporal and even ultimate happiness depend completely on your wish, on your own mind. Different results come from different types of wishes. All suffering arises from the misguided wish for your own temporal happiness in only this life. This kind of happiness seems to be happiness, but it is really only suffering. This is samsaric happiness, which cannot be found because it does not exist. However, from the wish to achieve liberation comes liberation. From the wish to achieve the omniscient, enlightened mind comes the omniscient, enlightened mind. Thus samsaric suffering and ultimate happiness come completely from your own wish, from your own mind.

If you closely examine your own experience, you will see that happiness and suffering are dependent upon your mind, upon your interpretation of events and circumstances. Happiness and suffering do not come from outside, from others. All of your happiness and all of your suffering are created by you, by your own mind and motivation.

You will experience suffering if you cultivate and indulge in anger, and you will experience happiness if you practice loving-kindness, compassion, and patience. Your suffering and happiness are the direct result of the way in which you take care of your own mind in your life on a day-to-day basis. If you closely examine your own experience, it becomes very clear that suffering and happiness are not created by other living beings, not even by a being such as God or Buddha. You are the creator of your own happiness and suffering.

Happiness and suffering are manifestations of emptiness

By recognizing the benefits of sufferings, you are able to identify sufferings as good, and this will bring you happiness. But this happiness depends entirely upon properly understanding the benefits of problems and then, on that basis, identifying problematic situations as good. It is not a question of will but of understanding. When you skillfully understand challenging situations in this way, you are then able to realize, "This situation is not a problem. I am not suffering; I am happy." As with the suffering we previously perceived and believed in, this happiness comes entirely from our own minds—there is not the slightest happiness existing anywhere else. The happiness that appears to exist externally, out there, is empty; it exists in dependence upon the nature of the feeling and the thought that labels it. Thus, happiness is a manifestation of emptiness.

It is the same with suffering. When you do not realize the benefits of problems but identify them only as interferences, you turn them into real problems, labeling them with the thought, "This is a problem." Your label causes the situation to then appear to you in a certain way. You have called it a problem, so it appears to you as a problem. The status of "problem" is merely imputed to that particular feeling by the thought that labels it. In reality, even though the problem appears to exist self-sufficiently—to exist "from its own side"—it is completely empty. Thus, you can see how suffering is also a manifestation of emptiness.

When you look at or think of your "self," of what you call "I," it appears to exist from its own side; you impute true, independent existence to the self, and to what are called the *aggregates*. The Buddha taught that a person is made up five components or aggregates—one material component (the body) and four mental ones, which include all our thoughts and emotions. Without the aggregates as the basis upon which the "I" is imputed, even if the thought that labels "I" arises, the "I" does not thereby exist. Conversely, in the absence of the thought that labels "I" on the basis of the aggregates, even if the aggregates are there, the "I" does not exist.

Thus, you can see that thought simply imputes a self to the mere appearance of the aggregates. And to the different activities performed by the aggregates, thought merely imputes, "I am sitting," "I am practicing Dharma," "I am meditating." Your mind imputes "I" to the aggregates performing these various activities. In reality, the self that seems to exist and do all these actions is merely ascribed to the aggregates—nothing more than this. Truly, the way the self exists is not the slightest bit more than this. In reality, the "I" is only what is merely imputed by thought on the basis of the aggregates.

And yet, even though the self is merely labeled by thought from its own side, it appears to exist as *more* than what is merely imputed by thought; it is, however, completely empty. Even though it appears to exist from its own side, this self-sufficient existence is just not there. It is a complete hallucination. Not even a single atom of the self has true, independent existence. The self that performs various activities, experiences samsara, and can achieve enlightenment through practicing Dharma is nothing more than what is merely imputed on the aggregates by thought. This is the self that does exist.

Now you can see very clearly that all the other ways the self appears to exist are complete illusions, complete hallucinations. This false self is what is referred to in the texts as the "object to be refuted." Any belief that the self exists in any way, other than as merely labeled on the basis of the aggregrates, should be abandoned.

This teaching has implications beyond the nature of the self. One of my teachers explained that the superstitious mind imputes a mere label to everything. All experiences, good or bad, are simply the gathering of causes and conditions. We label our experiences, and the mere label that we have imputed then appears to exist from its own side, independent of our mind. In reality, nothing exists from its own side; nothing exists independently. Everything is empty of existing from its own side. What this means is that there is no point at all in becoming attached or angry in response to anything that occurs. Because our experiences are empty of existing in this way, we don't have to experience them as problems. We can totally abandon disturbing thoughts.

4

The Shortcomings
of Anger and Desire

You follow desire,

and you are not satisfied.

Again you follow desire,

and again you are not satisfied.

Again you try,

and again you are not satisfied.

Following anger

FROM YOUR OWN EXPERIENCE, you know that there is no mental peace when you do not control your mind, when you follow anger. There is peace, however, when you apply Dharma meditations and teachings in your daily life, controlling your mind by practicing patience, loving-kindness, and compassion. It is especially important to practice patience, loving-kindness, and compassion in dangerous circumstances, the ones that can cause disturbing negative thoughts to arise. This is not easy in the beginning, but as with any skill, it can be developed with practice and familiarization.

The first step is to become aware when your mind is becoming disturbed, when you are feeling threatened or angry. As soon as anger begins to arise, you need to recognize it. Once you are aware of it, you then consciously and systematically recollect its shortcomings: Anger never brings the slightest benefit or happiness to you or to others; anger brings only harm, making you unhappy, disturbed, even vengeful and vicious. When you allow yourself to be controlled by anger, that anger deeply affects your mind; it leaves an imprint on your mind, and the next time you meet similar conditions, anger easily arises again out of habit. If you don't practice Mahayana thought transformation in these dangerous circumstances, every time you get angry, you pave the way for more and more anger to arise in the future.

Anger obscures your mind and makes your life unhappy. Anger can cause physical harm and even endanger your life. When you are angry, you are certainly unhappy and may be afraid, and you may also cause fear and unhappiness in others. Anger can make you destructive. With anger you become capable of harming the possessions, minds, bodies, and even lives of others. While your anger is strong, it is difficult to think of anything other than the wish to harm. You may wish to immediately destroy the object of your anger. And once this thought has arisen, it takes only a moment of action to harm, even kill, other beings. It does not take long to inflict great harm in such a state of mind—a mere moment is enough.

Anger causes you and others great problems every moment in which it arises in your life; and it continues to cause harm endlessly into the future. The state of enlightenment depends on an immense collection of virtuous activity, or merit. Anger prevents the achievement of liberation and the state of enlightened, omniscient mind by destroying that merit.

When the heart stops, life is cut off; like this, anger destroys the heart of merit and so cuts off the life of liberation. Without the heart, there is no life; without merit, there is no happiness, no liberation, no peerless, ultimate happiness of enlightenment.

Anger is extremely harmful. The scriptures explain at great length how anger destroys the happiness of future lives. But, for this practice, it is not necessary to even consider the effect on future lives; the problems anger causes in this life are immense. In this life alone, your anger continually harms you and so many beings.

The antidote to anger is patience. Each angry thought must be countered with a patient thought, for the angry thought itself cannot recollect the drawbacks of anger. We can only remember the shortcomings of anger by practicing patience. By applying the meditations and teachings of Mahayana thought transformation, you practice patience. When you apply them successfully, immediately there is tranquillity, relaxation, and much happiness in your life.

The pain of anger is like burning red-hot coals in your heart. Anger transforms even a beautiful person into something dark, ugly, and terrifying. As soon as you apply the teachings and practice patience, however, anger stops; and as soon as it stops, even your appearance suddenly changes. You appear different, and things appear different to you. You become peaceful and happy, your warm-hearted, loving nature makes others happy as well.

Following desire

As with anger, as long as you cling to and follow desire, there can be no lasting happiness or peace in your heart. Something is always missing. If you examine your mind carefully in any given moment, you will see that something is missing. This is true all the time. No matter how much you try to enjoy different places—living in a city or on a mountain, going to the beach or to a beautiful park—no matter how much you try to enjoy food, clothing—anything that can be obtained on this earth—there is always the feeling in your heart that something is lacking. No matter how many friends you have or how long you enjoy their company, there is always something missing. All the time there is something missing in your heart. You are never perfectly happy.

Even in moments of excitement, if you carefully examine your mind, you will discover the feeling that something is still missing and you are not perfectly content. Watch your mind closely; examine it well. Ask yourself: "Is this happiness complete or not? Am I still looking for something more?" You will always find that there is still something missing, that you are looking for something more.

This is why Buddha taught that no matter where you live, it is a place of suffering; no matter what enjoyment you have, it is the enjoyment of suffering; no matter what friend you are with, you are also with suffering. No matter what we experience, we are experiencing suffering.

As long as you cling to and follow desire, there can be no satisfaction. You imagine that following desire will bring satisfaction—that's the reason you do it. But although the aim is to gain satisfaction, because following desire is a flawed means of attaining ultimate happiness, the result is only dissatisfaction—this is all it can ever be. You follow desire, and you are not satisfied. Again you follow desire, and again you are not satisfied. Again you try, and again you are not satisfied.

It is like the life story of Elvis Presley. I learned about his life when I was in Melbourne once. While eating lunch one day, we watched the story of Elvis on TV. It was very interesting. His whole life story was a very effective Dharma teaching. In both his early and later life he enjoyed much pleasure and excitement, with fame and wealth and everything that brings. Then, in his final year of life, when he sensed he was soon going to die, he became deeply depressed. The words of the last song he chose to sing were: "I tried and I tried, but I can't get no satisfaction." During his last concert, tears streamed from his eyes as he sang, and the thousands of fans who were watching him and listening to his song also cried.

If you examine your mind while you are following desire, you will find there is always something missing. Actually, following desire in itself is suffering; following desire in itself is a problem. Suffering is in the very nature of following desire. No matter how much you follow desire, you do not gain satisfaction. You will only find dissatisfaction. In samsara, this dissatisfaction is the source of most suffering.

What causes problems and obstacles in life? What causes the many internal and external obstacles to your spiritual practice? What makes you unable to succeed in your Dharma practice? The answer is simple: following desire and not finding satisfaction. So many disasters in so many people's lives come from following desire and not finding satisfaction.

If you diligently examine your mind, analyzing and questioning yourself continually, you will find that as long as you follow desire, there is no real happiness. Something big is always missing. Your life is always empty.

In reality, both having the object of your desire and not having it are by nature suffering. Having the object is suffering; not having it is suffering. If you don't examine your mind carefully, you may believe that obtaining an object of desire seems to stop a problem: the problem of not having the particular object you want. If you follow your desire and get that object, then the problem of not having that object has stopped. But other problems start.

When the problem of not having an object of desire is stopped by obtaining the object, we impute "pleasure" to the change of feeling that arises when we come into contact with the object of desire. With continuing contact between our senses and the object, however, sooner or later the pleasurable feeling becomes unpleasurable, and is seen as an unbearable problem. Buddhism calls impermanent pleasures the "suffering of change," while unpleasant and painful experiences are called the "suffering of suffering."

Until you recognize and label the feeling as a problem, until you identify it as the suffering of suffering, you impute "pleasure" to the experience of having sense contact with an object you have labeled "desirable." Because you have called it "pleasure," the feeling appears as pleasure— seeming even to exist as pleasure from its own side. In other words, although the feeling is only labeled "pleasure," the pleasure appears to exist inherently.

But it is only a question of time before continuous contact between sense and object becomes unbearable. Your mind imputes "pleasure" to that feeling for a while, but eventually you come to recognize sustained sense contact with it as discomfort, the obvious suffering of suffering. It seemed like pleasure turned into suffering, but in reality, it was always suffering. Whenever we encounter any object or situation, one of three types of feeling is experienced, all of which are suffering. If we identify the object or situation as a problem, we will experience a feeling of suffering. If we identify an object or situation as desirable, we will experience a feeling of pleasure, but even this feeling of pleasure, when examined fully, is suffering. Finally, if we encounter an object that is neither desirable nor undesirable, a feeling of indifference will arise, and this too is ultimately suffering.

Every encounter with samsara and the objects of samsara leads only to suffering. This is because the aggregates themselves, the mind and body, are contaminated by the seeds of past karma and disturbing thoughts. As long as you are bound to samsara by past karma and disturbing thoughts you will experience suffering continuously. Every feeling that arises when you meet a sense object, even if it superficially appears pleasurable or neutral, is, in its deeper nature, suffering.

Following desire compounds negative karma, leaving an imprint in your mind that causes you to create more samsaric suffering in the future. Then, in the future, still under the control of past karma and delusions, you again have to experience the pervasive suffering of samsara because of your past actions. Because of following desire in the past, you have to experience the suffering of suffering, as well as the suffering of change—the temporary pleasures of samsara. This is the long-term harm of clinging to and following desire. As long as you follow desire, you experience suffering not only in the present, but you also ensure that you will endlessly experience the sufferings of samsara on into the future.

It is important then to realize that even the feeling that arises when you come into contact with an object of desire, which you label "pleasure," is only a form of suffering. When you do not analyze the true nature of this feeling, your deluded, hallucinating mind imputes "pleasure" to that feeling, which is in reality only suffering. Because of your delusion, because of your hallucination, the suffering feeling appears to you as pleasure, and you believe that it really is pleasure. You grasp on to that, and it appears to your hallucinating mind as pure, truly existent happiness. In this way all suffering comes from your own mind. To attain ultimate and lasting happiness, you must cut off desire at its root.

Cutting off desire

When you are experiencing huge mountains of problems that seem impossible to bear, if you are somehow able to identify that you have caused these problems by clinging to and following desire, you will stop following desire, and immediately your mountains of problems will disappear.

For example, while you are constantly thinking of how beautiful someone's body is, you certainly cannot stop desire. As long as you are thinking in this way, trying to stop attachment, to cut off your desire, is exhausting and useless. In fact, it only causes you to develop more attachment. It is impossible to stop desire in this way.

The thought that exaggerates the beauty of a person cannot stop attachment. The only thought that can stop this kind of attachment is thought that recognizes the nature of the body as suffering, as impermanent, and as an unappealing collection of flesh, bones, blood, and so on. You may feel: "I'm the only person in the world who has problems like this!" or "I have the biggest problems in the world!" This bleak, exaggerated view of everything is immediately stopped when you cut off desire. Recognizing that the root of all your problems is following desire, you can stop following desire by relying on the remedy, the Dharma teachings of thought transformation. If you can apply these teachings, immediately you experience tranquillity and great satisfaction—right then, right in the instant you apply the teachings. By seeing the shortcomings of desire, you stop your problems, you cut them off at the root. When you can do this, you will experience satisfaction and happiness in your daily life, and you will experience liberation. Cutting off desire liberates you.

In the ceremony of taking refuge in Buddha, Dharma, and Sangha, the prayer of refuge in Dharma says: "I go for refuge to the supreme cessation of attachment." The reason the cessation of attachment is particularly mentioned rather than the cessation of anger or another disturbing thought is that all sufferings are the result of desire. If you do not renounce desire, your suffering in samsara has no end. It does not matter what others do. If they cease following desire, they will be liberated. And if you stop following desire, you will be liberated as well.

Just as exaggerating the beauty of something cannot stop attachment, similarly perceiving as problems the harm you receive or the difficulties that arise will never stop suffering. The more you see problems as problems, the more unbearable they will become. It is impossible to stop suffering by thinking in this way; identifying problems as suffering only makes your suffering more and more unbearable.

Instead, leave the mind in its natural, undisturbed state. Don't follow thoughts of "This is a problem, that is a problem." Without labeling difficulties as problems, leave your mind in its natural state. In this way, you will stop seeing miserable conditions as problems.

5

Transforming Your
Problems into the Path

Recognizing undesirable

situations as desirable

is one of the most powerful

thought-training practices.

It is the way to transform

suffering into happiness.

TRANSFORMING MISERABLE CONDITIONS into necessary conditions that help us move along the path to enlightenment has great benefit, especially in the exceptionally difficult times in which we live.

In these difficult times, obstacles to practicing Dharma and achieving ultimate happiness are so numerous that you simply cannot avoid them. There are certain problems—such as having many demands on our time, or being sick, and ultimately dying—that we will inevitably experience. We have no choice. When these circumstances arise, you must be able to transform miserable conditions and unwanted obstacles into beneficial and necessary conditions that further your Dharma practice and help bring ultimate happiness. If you cannot make use of every condition that arises, both undesirable and desirable, you are in danger of losing the Dharma, and you will never achieve the unsurpassed and lasting happiness of enlightenment.

There is the danger of losing the Dharma even when you encounter desirable conditions. A Mahayana thought-training teaching says:

> It is not good to be wealthy; it is better to be poor. If you
> are poor and experience hardships, you can accomplish the
> Buddhadharma. The beggar's body is the aim of the Dharma.

Many famous Buddhist teachers, such as the great lama Milarepa, achieved enlightenment by leading an ascetic life. What does it mean to lead an ascetic life? From this verse, it may sound as if you have to become an actual beggar, but it does not mean that. Rather, the point is to cut off worldly concern, to dismantle the very foundation of all obstacles to completing Dharma practice and achieving ultimate happiness.

This teaching goes on to say:

> It is not good to be praised; it is better to be criticized. It is not good to have comfort; it is better to have discomfort. If you have comfort, you exhaust the merit accumulated in past times. Experiencing problems is the blessing of the guru.

When you are praised, or have earned a good reputation or an important position, again there is danger of losing the Dharma. When desirable conditions arise and you are happy because everything is going exactly the way you want it to, there is danger of losing the Dharma. Furthermore, because you worry about the passing of these desirable conditions, you are in danger of losing the Dharma. And then, when your desirable conditions pass, as they inevitably will, and you meet the opposite, undesirable situation, there is also danger of losing the Dharma.

It is very difficult to practice the Dharma. If you lose even what small amount of thought transformation you attempt or pretend to do, your life will become extremely poor. Whether conditions are bad or good, easy or hard, desirable or undesirable, you need to be able to transform them so that they cannot hinder your Dharma practice and your journey to enlightenment. Problems help you to achieve enlightenment.

When you have a problem, think: "This is the blessing of the Buddha. This situation is purifying me by exhausting my negative karma and by helping me to train my mind in Mahayana thought transformation so that I can achieve enlightenment for the sake of all beings. I welcome this problem as an opportunity for me to train my mind."

You cannot stop your suffering by identifying as a problem some harm that has come to you or some undesirable situation that has arisen, and then thinking over and over again that the condition is a problem. When you encounter an undesirable situation, a thought arises that interprets your experience as a problem, and this causes suffering. The only way to stop that suffering is to give rise to another thought that recognizes and interprets your experience as happiness. Only this thought can stop that suffering, only this thought can quell the unhappy mind.

Therefore, whenever a problem arises, you can be happy by recognizing it as beneficial, by seeing that it supports the generation of the path to enlightenment and ultimate happiness within your mind. Rejoice each time you meet an obstacle. Immediately think: "This appears to be an obstacle, but actually it is not an obstacle. Actually this is supporting the generation of enlightenment within me." Enjoy the obstacle; be happy.

When you meet miserable conditions, it is extremely important to use your mind skillfully, to employ the skillful means of the Dharma teachings. There is always a meditation to mix with whatever suffering you experience. Not every problem should be approached the same way. For one problem, apply one method; for another problem, apply a different method. When you are able to apply the teachings skillfully in this way, all sufferings can be mixed with virtue. In fact, all experiences of suffering become virtue.

Accepting problems rather than rejecting them can make a big difference to your experience, helping temporarily to stop worry and fear. On top of this, if you can mix your problems with virtue by applying Mahayana thought transformation, your experience of problems will actually become Dharma. You can use problems to generate what are called the three principal aspects of the path within your mind. All the Buddha's teachings and the entire path to enlightenment are condensed within these three aspects: the renunciation of samsara, *bodhichitta*—the wish to liberate all beings—and the realization of emptiness. Using problems in this way becomes a cause of happiness. Experiencing any problem exhausts particular past negative karma, but transforming the experience of the problem into virtue results in happiness.

Think extensively and repeatedly of the great benefit you receive from suffering. Outline each skillful means. It is very important to think in detail of the benefits of problems, since this is the main method of generating with increasingly greater strength and determination the thought of liking miserable conditions. Recognizing undesirable situations as desirable is one of the most powerful thought-training practices you can do. This is the way to transform suffering into happiness.

Using problems to train your mind in renunciation

Problems are just another form of teaching. Problems give you the clearest introduction to Dharma, and clear opportunity to renounce samsara. Because problems demonstrate so effectively how the nature of samsara is only suffering, problems make it easier for you to quickly generate renunciation, the first of the three principal aspects of the path to enlightenment. Samsara means the cycle of desire and dissatisfaction—birth, death, and rebirth—that is fueled by karma and delusions. By renouncing samsara, we renounce our habitual grasping, unhappy minds. By renouncing samsara, we embrace our potential for enlightenment.

When you have a problem, think like this: "As long as I wander in samsara without freedom, controlled by karma and delusions, the suffering that I experience is suffering I have created, not something that I do not deserve. This is the nature of samsara." When you think like this about whatever problem you experience—failure in retreat, sickness, relationship problems—the fear and worry about the problem will immediately decrease and ultimately disappear. You will feel less irritated and much more relaxed. Your problem will not seem so unbearable or even as big. In this way, an unbearable problem becomes bearable.

When you have a problem, think of all the suffering that exists among human beings. Think of the people who have many more or much greater problems than you have. You may be sick, but some people not only have a disease but one that is difficult to cure or incurable. You may not like your work, but some homeless people cannot find a job at all. You may be having difficulty in your relationships, but think of pregnant or sick or dying people with nobody at all to take care of them; of deserted husbands and wives; of children whose parents have problems with alcohol or drug abuse. In every family there are many problems. Every person always has some particular problems of their own. Think of the people who live amid war, starvation, and destruction.

Think also of all the beings who have not met the Dharma, and the people who have no freedom to practice the Dharma. These people do not even have the means to create the cause of happiness and abandon the cause of suffering.

When you think of other people with greater problems, your own problems seem very small and bearable. And when your big problems become small, it is even easier to see your small problems as almost pleasurable. When you think in this way, you no longer dislike miserable conditions. That feeling of aversion disappears.

Remember that samsara is a depthless ocean of suffering. Know that samsara arises because your aggregates, your mind and body, are contaminated by the seed of past karma and delusions. Because you have not generated within your mind the remedy, the true path and the true cessation of suffering, you are still bound by past karma and delusions. Because you are bound by past karma and past delusion, attachment arises when you meet a desirable object, and anger or aversion arises when you meet an undesirable object.

Delusions arise because you have not removed the imprints left by past deluded thoughts by generating in your mind the remedy. Delusions only arise when you have not applied the teachings of the Dharma and have not practiced Mahayana thought transformation in order to control your mind.

As explained in the teachings on the wheel of life, a disturbing thought arises and motivates the compounding karma that causes your continuing existence in samsara, your physical and mental aggregates. So, this life is the product of your past karma and disturbing thoughts, and disturbing thoughts in the present cause your deluded mind to pass from one moment to the next, from one life to the next. Until you cease creating the negative karma and disturbing thoughts that tie you to samsara, your suffering body and mind will arise continually from moment to moment, from life to life.

Don't point to some external thing and call it samsara; point to your own mind, your own body, and remember, "This samsara is the depthless ocean of suffering." By thinking in this way, generate aversion to samsara and turn your mind toward liberation. Mix the problem you are experiencing with the Dharma, with Mahayana thought transformation. Thinking that suffering is the very nature of samsara causes the thought of renunciation of samsara to develop. By renouncing samsara, you mix your deluded mind with virtue.

When you experience problems, it is also very good to think: "This is nothing. This problem is child's play."

No matter what disaster you experience, even if somebody steals all your belongings—clothing, money, everything; even if you have a heart attack; even if your wife, husband, or all your friends leave you; even if the worst situation imaginable comes to pass—think: "This is nothing; this is child's play. I have accumulated so much negative karma in the past that, of course, I experience problems. Because I have created the cause, these problems must arise. I will inevitably experience the result of karma I have created. This is the nature of samsara; it is nothing to be depressed about. This problem is like a great pleasure for me. There are much heavier problems still to come."

Thinking of the heavier problems still to come makes your present problem seem smaller. This is the psychology. Actually, all the teachings of the Dharma and of Mahayana thought transformation are extremely profound psychological methods designed to completely remove the cause of even the smallest suffering. When practiced thoroughly the Dharma completely removes not only negative karma and disturbing thoughts, but even the subtle imprints of these left in your mind, and thus leads you to the peerless happiness of enlightenment. Buddhist psychology is extremely skillful at leading people to the state of enlightened, omniscient mind.

Using problems to train your mind in refuge

You can use your problems to strengthen your refuge, to strengthen your reliance upon Buddha, Dharma, and Sangha.

Think of all the sufferings you have experienced. The only refuge that gives you perfect protection is the Triple Gem—the Buddha, Dharma, and Sangha. Because samsaric pleasure and relief are only temporary, they are not reliable refuges. But the Triple Gem opens us to our mind's potential for true liberation, true freedom and lasting happiness, and so can never let us down. So think: "No matter what problems occur in my life, I'm going to rely only on the Triple Gem."

All suffering of samsara comes from the same true causes: ignorance and disturbing thoughts. Disturbing thoughts motivate negative karma, which leaves imprints in the mind, which in turn give rise to future lives and future experiences of suffering. Again and again in every moment and every life, you experience the suffering of birth and death. Since beginningless time, so much karma has been created, and you carry within your mind the causes for so much future suffering.

You must think: "There are uncountable results of past karma I have yet to experience, oceans of samsaric suffering. Only the Triple Gem has the power to liberate me from all true suffering and the true cause of suffering. And since the Triple Gem has the power to liberate me completely from all samsara, why not from these problems that I am experiencing now? Therefore, no matter how difficult my life is, I won't give up refuge in the Triple Gem. No matter how many problems I have, I won't give up Buddha, Dharma, and Sangha." Use your problems in this way to train your mind in refuge and strengthen your reliance upon the Buddha, Dharma, and Sangha.

Using problems to eliminate pride

Whenever you experience problems, use them to eliminate pride, one of the five primary delusions. Until you completely liberate yourself from delusions, you have no real freedom and are continually affected by past karma and disturbing thoughts, and you constantly experience the suffering of change and the suffering of suffering. In addition, you will also experience the pervasive compounding suffering that keeps us locked in samsara. Remembering this, think: "I'm going to cut off pride, the enemy that destroys myriad good qualities. I'm going to cut off this evil self-cherishing thought that is careless of other living beings." Pride seems to be our friend, but in reality it only brings us endless problems. By remembering this, we will immediately want to rid ourselves of this attitude.

Pride focuses on the problems of others and exaggerates your own good qualities. When you realize that you yourself have many problems, and you recollect them, pride does not arise. Recognizing your own suffering eliminates pride and causes compassion to arise toward others who, like you, are suffering in samsara. With pride, you rejoice when others have problems, and this prevents compassion from arising. If you instead recollect your own problems, then the virtuous mind of wanting the happiness of others arises easily.

A thought-training teaching mentions:

It is not good to be praised; it is better to be criticized.
When you are praised, great pride arises. When you are
criticized, your own mistake is blown away.

One of the benefits of criticism is that it immediately destroys pride; it negates the unskillful thought of pride. Free from pride, you are able to make true progress in your life.

Likewise if you are praised, pride will arise too. When pride arises, negative karma is created. If you let pride arise, you will experience the result of rebirth in realms where there is no freedom to practice Dharma. When pride arises, even though you may have great aspirations, you will have little capability to do anything for your own ultimate happiness or for the happiness of others. Ultimately, you will not succeed.

You cannot develop your mind and attain ultimate happiness if you allow pride to arise. You cannot even properly learn about Dharma. Your mind is a like a balloon, and the healing Dharma is like water. When your mind swells up with pride, no Dharma can get in. You must empty your mind of pride to receive the Dharma.

The great Kadampa masters explain that all the teachings of Buddha are meant to destroy pride. One way to control pride is to contemplate your own mistakes. Thinking of your successes causes pride to arise; but when you look at your mistakes, pride disappears from your mind. Consider how little you know. Consider whatever worldly knowledge you may possess and even whatever small knowledge of the Dharma you may have, then consider how little this knowledge has helped you attain ultimate happiness and consider how much more you have to learn. There are subjects you may feel you know—you may know the words, but you do not have the realizations. Although you may understand the explanations, if you are still suffering because of problems, you clearly do not understand the true nature of your mind, your body, and your senses. Thinking in this way helps to stop pride.

The benefits of rejoicing

The practice of rejoicing can prevent the arising of pride, jealousy, or anger. Whenever you hear that someone else has been successful, rejoice. Always practice rejoicing for others—whether your friend or your enemy—even about samsaric success. For example, when you hear that someone has been successful in business, you should rejoice. When you hear that someone has found a partner, again rejoice. You should think: "How wonderful it is that they have found the happiness they were seeking!" Practice feeling as happy for others as you do for yourself. In other words, cherish others as you cherish yourself. Feel happy when others find happiness, as if you yourself had found happiness.

If you cherish only yourself, you cannot experience happiness, but if you cherish others as you cherish yourself, happiness arises naturally. When you cherish others as you cherish yourself, if someone finds the happiness they were seeking, you naturally feel happy, without any need to think of reasons. When something good happens to anyone, you naturally feel happy.

Every positive trait is the result of past good actions, and all can be a basis for you to rejoice. When you see someone possessed of physical beauty, think: "How wonderful it is that this person has a beautiful body now as a result of practicing patience and morality in past lives." When you see someone who is very wealthy, think: "How wonderful it is that this person is experiencing the good karma resulting from giving to other beings and making offerings to the Triple Gem in the past." If someone is very intelligent or has more understanding of Dharma than you do, you can rejoice in this as well. And if someone has done many meditation retreats, even if you have not had the chance to do any, rejoice for them and the good karma they have created.

Simply by rejoicing, without the need for extensive preparation or any special effort, you can accumulate incredible merit, incredible good karma. In one second you can accumulate merit infinite as space. If you really practice it honestly, rejoicing in others is the easiest way to accumulate extensive merit and attain ultimate happiness.

Furthermore, immediately rejoicing when you find good qualities in others also stops feelings of jealousy. When you feel jealous, you may have the unskillful wish to interfere with the success and happiness of others. But if you abandon jealousy and practice rejoicing, even though you yourself may not be successful now, you create the cause to be successful and happy in the future. By rejoicing now when others are able to do much Dharma practice and retreat and gain understanding and realizations, you create the cause to have these experiences yourself later.

Allowing pride and jealousy to arise creates only obstacles to success both now and in the future—obstacles not only to practicing Dharma and developing your mind, but even to success in the worldly activities of this life. Rejoicing is a skillful psychological method to achieve happiness and a very important part of everyday life. You will find that rejoicing when others achieve samsaric success and find the happiness they seek solves many of your own problems.

On the other hand, if you do not practice rejoicing, if you do not practice exchanging yourself with others, then no matter how many years you have this precious human body and these precious opportunities to practice Dharma, no matter how much wealth, intelligence, or worldly or Dharma education you have, there can be no lasting happiness or peace in your life. Ultimately, it is the inability to rejoice in others that causes depression and makes people crazy. If you cannot rejoice in others, no matter how long you live, you will be unhappy and do crazy things.

Because you have this precious gift of a human body and because you have the buddha-potential within your heart, you have the ability to bring tremendous and lasting benefit to yourself and to all other living beings. But if you do not apply these Dharma practices in your daily life, you will have cut off all these benefits.

Using problems to purify negative karma

Another benefit of having problems is that you can use them to purify negative karma. Think: "All my problems come only from my negative karma." This may sound heavy, but remember if our problems come from our own karma and not from the outside, then we can eliminate our problems by eliminating our negative karma. Remember the four properties of karma and apply them to your present problems. The four properties of karma are that karma is definite; karma can expand; one cannot experience a result without having created its cause; and once created, karma is never lost.

We can apply our knowledge of these four properties to any problem that arises in our lives. Take, for example, the experience of disharmony in a relationship. This can arise due to having engaged in some form of sexual misconduct in the past. When there are many problems and quarrels in your relationship, you can think about them in terms of karma.

Think in this way: "I have created negative karma, so I will *definitely* experience its results. The reason I have been experiencing these problems again and again for such a long time is that karma can *expand,* it can grow with time if it is not purified. Everything in my life now has a *cause;* for instance, from committing sexual misconduct in the past, my relationship is full of quarrels now, and if I had practiced the perfections of virtue and morality in the past, my life now would be happy and harmonious. Because I have not created this good karma and have instead created bad karma, I am suffering now."

Finally, remember that karma is *never lost.* Even though it may be one hundred eons before you experience the results, the karma you have accumulated never disappears. When the right time and perfect conditions occur, the karma will ripen and you will experience its effects.

What do we do then, knowing that, even if we do not create any new negative karma, we still have to experience the eons of negative karma that we've already created? If karma expands and is never lost, what can we do to prevent ourselves from experiencing the results? The answer is purification, which burns away the negative karmic seeds and prevents them from bearing fruit. There are many purification practices, but they are all based on the practice of the four opponent powers: the power of the basis, the power of regret, the power of the remedy, and the power of resolve.

So, think: "In the past, I did not purify my negative karma with the four opponent powers and did not apply the appropriate Dharma practice. Since I did not apply the appropriate practice, I have not created any conditions to prevent my experiencing the results of this karma. Because I did nothing to counteract my negative karma, I am now experiencing the results." In this way, apply your knowledge of the four properties of karma to your present problem.

Think to yourself: "This problem is a teaching for me. It is teaching me that if I don't like this problem, I must abandon its cause, my own nonvirtue." With regard to any past negative karma, the first thing to do is to purify by applying the four opponent powers, and then abstain from committing the negative karma again. In this way, the problem becomes an extremely beneficial teaching.

Milarepa was a great Tibetan saint, but before he became enlightened he used black magic to kill many people and animals. Milarepa felt: "I am a very evil person. I must confess and purify all this and practice Dharma." With the strong wish to practice Dharma, Milarepa went to meet his future teacher, Marpa, and he became enlightened in that lifetime through rigorous purification and Dharma practice.

There are many similar stories of people who, after experiencing some heavy problem, got completely fed up with their worldly life, sought out a teacher, received teachings, and then practiced diligently for a long while. They practiced diligently and then achieved enlightenment and ultimate happiness. This has happened many times, to many people: lay people, monks, and nuns. In the beginning, they had no intention to dedicate their lives completely to Dharma, but then the experience of some heavy problem caused them to generate complete renunciation of delusion and samsara. People like this become very pure Dharma practitioners, practicing despite many hardships and achieving very high realizations of the path.

But you must not abstain only from creating heavy negative karma; you must abandon even the smallest negative actions, the smallest negative thoughts. You desire not only great enjoyments, but even the smallest comfort, even in your dreams. And besides not wanting big problems, you do not want even the smallest discomfort; you do not want even an unpleasant dream. Therefore, you must cease creating even the smallest negative karma.

Using problems as an inspiration to practice virtue

Through your problems you can come to like virtue. It is said that, "Miserable conditions persuade you to practice virtue." One of my teachers explained that problems act as a warning: If you do not like suffering, you must abandon negative actions, purify past negative karma, and create good karma. While you are experiencing a problem, what you actually want is happiness, which is the absence of that problem, so you must think: "If I want happiness, if I desire the the absence of this problem, I must create the cause for happiness and the cause for the absence of this problem." In this way you use everyday problems as teachings, as reminders. Problems inspire you to create virtue, the cause of happiness.

If your life is free of problems and is utterly comfortable, you may become complacent and you may not remember to practice Dharma. Problems, such as being unjustly accused or suffering sickness or a loss, prevent complacency; they cause you to renounce samsara and attempt to practice virtue.

Just as you should abandon even the smallest negative thought, so should you strive to accomplish even the smallest virtue. The opportunities to accomplish virtues are countless, and whenever an opportunity presents itself to you, you should take it. As much as you can, cherish all beings around you with a good heart, and try to benefit them by giving them whatever help they need. Give them every single thing you can to make them happy: even a few sweet words or some interesting conversation that benefits their minds, that stops their problems even for a moment and makes them happy. Use every opportunity, every action of your body, speech, and mind, to increase your virtue.

Using problems to train your mind in compassion and loving-kindness

Problems give you the opportunity to train your mind in compassion. Everyone accepts that compassion as a good thing. Even people who have no understanding of karma recognize that compassion is a good thing.

In order to cultivate compassion, think of the many beings who are experiencing problems similar to yours and also of those who are experiencing more or greater problems. Even if they have the same problem, it may be a greater hardship for them to bear, or they may be experiencing many other problems as well.

Think: "Just as I want happiness and do not want suffering, everyone else also wants happiness and does not want suffering. In this way, we are all exactly the same. How good it would be if all these beings were freed from all their sufferings." Furthermore, take this opportunity to generate the mind of a bodhisattva, and think: "I will free them from all their sufferings." Use your problems in this way to train your mind in great compassion.

When you feel anger at the way others are treating you, remember the following verse by Shantideva in his *Guide to the Bodhisattva's Way of Life:*

My karma induced me to receive this harm. But didn't I harm
this person by causing them to be lost in the pit of the hells?

You receive harm from a particular person in a particular situation because in the past, in some way, you created a link with them by harming them. That karma then causes them to harm you now. Now, this person is creating negative karma by harming you, and this negative karma causes them to fall down into the pit of the hells, into unimaginable suffering. By having forced this other person to create this negative karma, to harm you now, you actually throw them into the hells.

If you can truly understand this verse and remember it when someone causes you problems, there is no possibility at all that anger will arise in your mind. Instead, compassion for the other person will arise naturally, without choice. Because you are motivated by compassion, you want only to help the person with every action, word, and thought, rather than to retaliate in anger. Compassion will motivate you to pacify their mind, to stop them from creating negative karma and help them to purify the negative karma they have already accumulated.

In a similar way, you can use your problems to train your mind in loving-kindness. When you have a problem, you are devoid of temporal and ultimate happiness. Remember all the other beings who are also without temporal and ultimate happiness. You and they are exactly the same in wanting happiness. Think: "How wonderful it would be if all living beings had happiness." Furthermore, think: "I myself will endeavor to cause each and every being to have happiness." This is a very powerful practice.

6

Experiencing Your
Problems for Others

Experience every single

undesirable thing

on behalf of all other

living beings.

*Using problems to generate bodhichitta
and to destroy self-cherishing*

PROBLEMS GIVE YOU THE OPPORTUNITY to train your mind in bodhichitta, the wish to become enlightened in order to free all beings from suffering. As your compassion for others grows, you increasingly come to feel that it is unbearable when any other being experiences suffering. Practicing bodhichitta—exchanging yourself for others—means renouncing yourself rather than others and cherishing others rather than yourself.

Unless you exchange yourself for others, you cannot become enlightened, and even in samsara you will never find happiness. Forget about the happiness of future lives; without bodhichitta, you will be eternally frustrated even in the activities of this life. No matter how how hard you strive toward happiness in your everyday life, you simply cannot experience it unless you develop a good, compassionate heart. Without a good heart, you will never have peace in your life.

The practice of bodhichitta is not only for those who seek enlightenment or the happiness of future lives; everyone will benefit from practicing it. The practice of bodhichitta does not require a belief in reincarnation or even in karma. Virtue results in happiness, nonvirtue in suffering. It's that simple—you can see for yourself, in your own experience.

If you want happiness—even just your own day-to-day happiness—you must practice the good heart, bodhichitta. This means exchanging yourself for others: renouncing yourself and cherishing others.

Even though bodhisattvas might experience problems as a result of past negative karma, they experience those problems for the sake of other living beings. They think, "By experiencing this problem, may I alleviate the suffering of others." Thus, instead of being problems, unfortunate events become sources of happiness; instead of being miserable conditions, they become happy conditions; instead of causing a miserable life, they cause a happy life. If you practice renouncing yourself and cherishing others, you can experience your problems for the sake of others. In this way, no matter what, you have a happy life. Problems do not disturb you; they only help you and all beings to actualize the path to enlightenment.

In order to achieve enlightenment for the sake of all living beings, you must destroy your enemy: the self-cherishing thought. This self-cherishing thought is the single greatest enemy to your own success, your own happiness, and that of all other beings. As long as self-cherishing dwells in your heart, there is no space to generate bodhichitta, so there is no way to achieve enlightenment and perfectly guide all living beings.

Following self-cherishing thoughts brings only pain, failure, and disharmony. The stronger your selfish mind, the stronger your anger, jealousy, attachment, and dissatisfaction. The more selfish you are, the more attachment and dissatisfaction you have, and thus the more difficulty you experience in your life, one thing after another.

Your selfish mind wants you to be the best. It wants you to be the smartest, most successful, most accomplished, most attractive. It wants you to be first among all others. Your selfish mind wants you alone to succeed and others to fail. And when the expectations of your selfish mind are not met, jealousy, anger, ill will, strong attachment, and other disturbing thoughts arise in force. Then, under the influence of these negative thoughts, you perform various unskillful, nonvirtuous actions and accumulate even more negative karma. If you follow self-cherishing thoughts, not only do you not experience even temporal happiness in that very moment, but as a result of this negative karma, you experience in the future only more of the suffering of suffering.

The less you practice exchanging yourself for others, and the stronger your selfish mind becomes, the more disturbing you will find people and situations. The more you cherish yourself and are concerned about only your own happiness and your own problems—"I have this problem, I have that problem. When will I be happy?"—the more you will experience misfortune and disturbing thoughts, and the more you will label these as problems.

Every time a problem arises, the essential thing is to immediately become aware that the problem comes from your selfish mind, that it is created by self-cherishing thoughts. Every time you have a problem, you should immediately try to see this process of evolution. As long as you put all the blame outside yourself, there can be no happiness. In reality, all the difficulties of life come from self-cherishing thoughts. Furthermore, all problems are the result of negative karma accumulated in the past due to self-cherishing thoughts. In the past, under the influence of self-cherishing, whenever you allowed disturbing thoughts to arise, these disturbing thoughts motivated negative karma. But you must understand that the problems you experience in your life now are related not only to past negative karma accumulated under the influence of the self-cherishing thought, but also to the self-cherishing thought in your mind at this very moment.

One of the most important things that Mahayana thought training teaches is putting all the blame on the self-cherishing thought, where it belongs. In this way you develop aversion to the self-cherishing thought and come to see it as your enemy. Thus, instead of identifying with and obeying the self-cherishing thought, you separate yourself from it—and then all your daily activities become pure Dharma practice.

No matter what difficult circumstances arise, put all the blame on the self-cherishing thought. Recollect how every difficulty is due to the shortcoming of self-cherishing. Then, on top of that, give back to the self-cherishing thought all the problems and undesirable things that the self-cherishing thought has given you. The self-cherishing mind wants you to look elsewhere for the source of your problems, but with this practice you lay the blame squarely on the root cause: self-cherishing itself.

Without this understanding, our problems cause us to create negative karma. But, by using your problems as weapons to destroy self-cherishing, whatever problem you are experiencing becomes a means to eliminate ignorance and negative karma. This is especially useful if the problem is unavoidable. By sending problems back to the self-cherishing thought and destroying it, your experience of problems really becomes Dharma practice.

Experiencing problems on behalf of others, exchanging yourself for others, is the practice of bodhichitta. There is no question that this is the most skillful, most effective way to purify your mind and attain the ultimate happiness of enlightenment. Even if you cannot do this practice, even if you cannot completely exchange yourself with others, you can still give every undesirable thing that happens to you back to the self-cherishing thought and destroy it. If you can do that, then every problem you experience becomes pure Dharma. Experiencing problems becomes the remedy to self-cherishing; experiencing problems becomes the very best Dharma practice. Using the difficulties in your life in this way becomes virtue. Even though you may not rely completely upon the Buddha, Dharma, and Sangha, even though you may not have faith in the law of karma, if you use your problems to destroy your own selfish mind, your own self-cherishing thoughts, you are practicing pure Dharma.

Whatever difficulties arise, put all the blame on your self-cherishing thoughts. Instead of thinking, "This is *my* problem," think "This is the problem of my self-cherishing thoughts"—and then destroy the self-cherishing by turning the problem back on it. Whatever energy you would have used to eliminate an external problem can now be used to eliminate your self-cherishing instead. It is especially effective to use your fears about being judged or criticized to destroy self-cherishing. If you can do this continually, then fears, worries, and paranoia cannot arise. This is the deep, essential psychology that really wipes out the self-cherishing thought, the source of all your problems, and makes it nonexistent.

There are inevitably many problems in your life that you will have to endure, that you have to experience again and again, that you have to learn to live with. Sickness, misfortunes, the infirmities of age, depression, anxiety, family problems, relationship issues, death of loved ones—many of these things are unavoidable. Some people are always being scolded or beaten by an alcoholic wife or husband. Whenever they are home, there is quarreling and fighting. They do not separate, and there is always unhappiness and disharmony in their lives. You may feel trapped in a heavy, awful situation of this kind and believe you have no escape; you may believe that the circumstances are difficult or impossible to change. Though you may not be able to change the external circumstances, you can change how you use your mind. One very effective thing you can do is to think: "All these problems have been given to me by my self-cherishing thought." Give all these problems back to your self-cherishing thought. And then decide to experience your problems on behalf of others. This is the bravest, most powerful practice you can do.

Think: "The reason that I have not yet been released from these problems is that from beginningless time I have cherished myself and renounced others. From now on, I'm going to live my life only with bodhichitta. I'm going to cherish others." Think this to yourself and know that this is the source of all happiness.

If you change your attitude from cherishing yourself to cherishing others, all your problems stop. All confusion is stopped simply by changing your attitude. This single practice of exchanging yourself with others stops all the confusion and every problem in your life.

Taking and giving

When you have a problem, another practice you can apply is the Mahayana thought-transformation practice of taking and giving *(tonglen)*. Visualize taking all the suffering of other beings into your own heart, and then imagine giving everything—your own body, possessions, happiness, and merit—to others. Many other beings have the same or similar problems as you do. Practice taking upon yourself their experience of those particular problems, as well as the suffering and causes of suffering of all other beings. Imagine that whatever problem you are experiencing is due to willingly taking upon yourself the problems of others, thereby relieving them of all suffering. In this way, you experience your problem for the benefit of others.

When you are able to think that you are experiencing your problems for other living beings, you transform your experience of those problems into virtue. Because you are experiencing your problem on behalf of all those with similar problems, as well as all those with other problems, your experience becomes great purification and a very skillful means to accumulate extensive positive potential. The number of beings for whom you experience the suffering is infinite, and thus you can develop infinite virtue.

Transforming illness into the path

Another thought transformation teaching says: "Disease is the broom that sweeps away negative karma and obscurations." Thus, you can feel happy when you become sick by thinking: "The fruit of the negative karma I've created in the past is ripening as this experience of sickness, in this life, at this moment. If I were not experiencing the results of my past negative karma now, the suffering I would experience in the future would be much greater. By experiencing it now, I have the opportunity to purify myself." Thinking like this allows you to live your life with a relaxed, happy mind. You do not get depressed or upset about your health, or about any problem. As your mind is relaxed, external conditions do not disturb you, and you are able to continue your Dharma practice; you are able to move closer to ultimate happiness.

Also think: "In the past I have practiced taking other beings' suffering upon myself and dedicating my body, possessions, happiness, and merits to others. Now I have received the sufferings, negative karma, and obscurations of others—so, therefore I have succeeded in my practice of taking and giving. My wish for the happiness of all beings has been granted." By thinking like this, you generate happiness.

One great teacher advised that when your disease gets worse and worse, you should think: "My illness indicates I have succeeded in my practice of giving and taking. By using my problems to practice taking and giving, I have developed great virtue, become the cause of happiness, and done much purification. If I were to recover instantly, I would lose this opportunity to practice Dharma. I wouldn't have any chance to practice the skillful means of taking and giving, which enables me to purify my obscurations and attain ultimate happiness. How fortunate I am that my problem has not stopped! If I didn't have this problem, I would become lazy. I would lose this precious opportunity to purify my past negative actions and develop great virtue."

As I mentioned before, you must not think that only this particular suffering of others has ripened upon you, whether it be cancer or losing a job, but rather think that *all* the sufferings of other beings have ripened upon you as well. Think: "I have received the present sufferings of all other beings and all the future sufferings they will have to experience until samsara ends. I am experiencing these on their behalf so that they may be completely free from suffering."

One of my teachers taught that we should also think: "How fantastic it is that I am actually able to take upon myself the sufferings of living beings at this time!" Rejoice and feel happy. Practicing taking and giving in this way is an opportunity to completely renounce yourself for others.

When you are doing an intensive meditation retreat on thought transformation, in the breaks between meditation sessions you should pray to be able to use your suffering in the Mahayana path. Then, when your mental capacity is more advanced you may actually choose to pray that you receive even more of the sufferings and problems of other beings. You may wish that all harms, all undesirable things—disease, failure, everything!—come to you rather than to others. You seek to experience all these bad conditions on behalf of other living beings.

Even if disturbing thoughts have arisen uncontrollably, or you have created negative karma through lapses in ethical conduct, use Mahayana thought transformation. Think: "While practicing taking and giving, I have been praying to receive upon myself all the undesirable experiences of other beings. Now my prayer has been answered. I am receiving all the undesirable experiences of others and experiencing them on their behalf."

Then pray: "May this negative karma represent the negative karma of all those who have transgressed their ethical commitments and have thereby cut off the root of liberation. May this negative karma substitute for every undesirable experience of every being. May I alone experience all the causes and all the suffering; may all other beings be free from all this negative karma and its results."

If you don't do your daily Dharma practice, for example, apply thought transformation in a similar way: "May this negative karma be a substitute for all the problems of all other beings. May I experience this karma on their behalf." Thus you can experience every single undesirable thing on behalf of all other living beings.

7

The Heart Advice

There is nothing to trust in

seeking happiness from outside;

you will only become

exhausted with suffering,

which is without satisfaction

and without end.

The power of the good heart

APPLYING EVEN ONE TECHNIQUE of Mahayana thought transformation is the best protection against suffering. For example, you can apply the teachings of this verse in the *Guru Puja,* a well-known practice text:

> Please grant me blessings to be able to take all the karmic debts,
> obstacles, and sufferings of other beings, without exception,
> upon myself and to dedicate my own body and merit to them.
> Thus, may I lead all beings to bliss.

If you are able to genuinely utilize this one verse in any situation, you will be constantly generating bodhichitta, renouncing yourself and cherishing others.

The practice of bodhichitta is your best protection. Practicing bodhichitta gives better protection than spending life after life for hundreds of eons learning to protect yourself with karate. The power of bodhichitta is incomparable. The power of atomic bombs is completely insignificant when compared to the power of one good heart.

Unless you change the way you use your mind, there will always be an enemy to harm you, there will always be unfortunate circumstances to befall you. But if all the people in the world truly possessed bodhichitta, we would have no need for guns, bombs, armies, and police. Lama Yeshe, my own precious teacher, used to say: "An apple a day keeps the doctor away; a good heart a day keeps the enemy away."

Imagine if, instead of putting all its effort into military development, a country were to put all its effort into the development of the mind, of the good heart! You might think that the country could be in danger from foreign powers. But truly, if the entire energy of everyone in a country were put into developing the good heart, there would be no danger from foreign powers—the power of the good heart is that great.

No matter how well developed its military power, a country can never be certain of defeating all its enemies all the time. It does not follow logically that having vast amounts of military personnel and equipment means that a country will attain even temporal success, temporal happiness. It is only when the entire emphasis of a country is on development of the mind and the good heart, with everyone accepting responsibility for their own heart and their own actions, that success comes. When that emphasis is lost, innumerable problems follow.

Take, for example, the Chinese in Tibet. I have not been to China; however, I have been twice to Tibet. Wherever you go in Tibet, it seems that the Chinese have put all their effort into military development. It reminds me of the way a dedicated meditator puts every single effort into striving to gain realizations of enlightenment: They eat, drink, and dress in order to train in the Dharma. They do everything to develop their mind, to achieve enlightenment for the sake of living beings.

Similarly, everywhere you go in Tibet—apart from some luxury hotels built for tourists—there is total concentration on developing military power. Everything is focused on this. The essence of Tibet—its mountains, its beauty—has been destroyed in order to develop military power. The main aim of having this power is to take over others, but in some ways, the happiness of even the Chinese people has been sacrificed. The lives of the Chinese in Tibet are completely concentrated on defeating others, and the services that would bring them comfort and happiness have been neglected.

When I visited eastern Tibet years ago, I stayed near the monastery of Kumbum in Amdo, where Lama Tsongkhapa was born. During my entire stay, I did not see any happiness at all in the people of that city. All the Chinese I met were unhappy. While traveling there, looking at the people, I reached the conclusion that there was not even one happy Chinese person to be found there.

The benefits of Mahayana thought transformation

When you are completely determined to practice Mahayana thought transformation, to use suffering and happiness in the Mahayana path, you cherish others and are able to completely sacrifice yourself; you are able to experience the sufferings of all beings by yourself alone. This is when real happiness starts. When you live your life opposing the self-cherishing thought, you are happy all the time. No matter what happens, no matter how the conditions of your life change, you are always able to be happy.

Training in Mahayana thought transformation makes your mind very flexible and light, and you develop a big heart. You are not easily disturbed. Other people feel comfortable in your company. There is happiness and courage in your heart. In every moment, day and night, wherever you go, your mind is fully confident, and you live in constant happiness. There are no obstacles to your Dharma practice, and all the conditions that once appeared miserable now appear auspicious. Everything appears as a good sign, as fortunate, and your mind is always content, happy, and peaceful.

In these difficult and dangerous times, there is no better armor, no better protection, than the practice of thought transformation. By doing these practices and not allowing yourself to be irritated by problems, you are suddenly released from all your problems, like an army dropping its weapons. You can even recover unexpectedly from serious illnesses.

When you practice Mahayana thought transformation, no living being, no circumstance or event can harm you—not even death. Even when you are dying, you are able to apply thought transformation and to practice giving and receiving. A person who is able to die with the thought of cherishing others is a compassionate person, a self-supporting person. If you die practicing taking and giving, with the thought of bodhichitta in your heart, you cannot have a lower rebirth. It is impossible. Without any difficulty and with complete joy in your heart, you will naturally be able to experience death for the benefit of all living beings.

Practicing in this way, you give yourself freedom all the time. This is what is meant by the meditative state of the bodhisattvas known as "all dharmas being pervaded by bliss."

The heart advice

The wise person, seeing that all happiness and suffering depend upon the mind, seeks happiness from the mind, not from anything external. The mind possesses all the causes of happiness, just as it possesses all the causes of suffering. You can see this in the practice of thought transformation, particularly when you use your sufferings in the path to enlightenment.

If you do not think of the benefits of problems—of mixing problems with Mahayana thought transformation and using them on the path to enlightenment for the benefit of all beings—but think only of the shortcomings of problems, you label difficulties as problems, and thus they then appear to you as problems, as totally undesirable. In this way, your mind creates your problems.

The cause of problems is your own mind; all problems come from your own mind. When you stop the thought of disliking problems and establish the thought of liking them, your problems appear as beneficial, wonderful things.

Any happiness you feel comes from your own mind. Every pleasure you experience—from the pleasantness of a cool breeze on a hot day, all the way to the ultimate happiness of enlightenment—all this comes from your own mind. It is all manufactured by your own inner factory.

All causes are there within your own mind. Since the thoughts within your mind are the causes of your happiness, seek happiness from your own mind. This is the most essential point of all the Buddha's teachings. Practicing thought transformation is the clearest, most skillful way to seek happiness from your own mind.

Your happiness does not depend on anything external. Even when someone is angry with you or acting maliciously toward you, by looking at them with compassion and loving-kindness from your heart, you can feel very warmly toward them, seeing them in the aspect of beauty. Using thought transformation, you can see that person as unbelievably precious and kind, as the most precious person in your life. Among all living beings, this angry, malicious person before you is the most precious, the most kind.

No matter what harm someone does to you with their body, speech, or mind—intentionally or unintentionally—by using thought transformation, you see what they are doing as only beneficial for developing your mind, and this makes you very happy. You can see very clearly that this happiness comes from your own mind; it does not depend on how others behave toward you or what they think of you.

What you think is a problem comes from your own mind; what you think is joyful comes from your own mind. Your happiness does not depend on anything external.

The foolish person seeks happiness outside, running around and keeping busy with that expectation. If you seek happiness outside yourself, you have no freedom, you always have problems, and you are never completely satisfied. You are unable to truly accomplish anything, unable to see reality clearly, and unable to judge correctly. If you seek happiness outside yourself, there are always so many problems. If you seek happiness outside yourself, there are always dangers, always enemies, always thieves. If you seek happiness from outside yourself, it is impossible to have complete satisfaction, complete success.

By seeking happiness outside yourself, you will only become exhausted with suffering, which is without satisfaction and without end. Within the many hundreds of different teachings on how to practice the Dharma, this is the heart advice.

⤳

You may have heard nothing new in this teaching. However, if you put this advice into practice, you will see definite and immediate benefits. If you do not try to practice this advice, even though you may have a library of Dharma teachings in your mind, your problems will continue and will continue to cause you suffering.

Mahayana thought transformation is the most powerful way to transform the problems of life into happiness. Try to put this teaching into practice as much as possible. This is the main thing.

Afterword

IN OCTOBER 1987 at Mahamudra Centre in New Zealand, Lama Thubten Zopa Rinpoche gave this commentary on the short thought-transformation text, *Instructions on Turning Happiness and Suffering into the Path of Enlightenment.* Compiled by the Third Dodrupchen Rinpoche, Jigme Tenpe Nyima (1865–1926), a great lama of the Nyingma order of Tibetan Buddhism, this text brings together advice from a variety of important Mahayana teachings, especially those of two of the greatest Indian Buddhist masters, Nagarjuna's *Ratnamala (The Precious Garland)* and Shantideva's *Bodhicharyavatara (Guide to the Bodhisattva's Way of Life).*

The teachings known as thought transformation *(lojong)* were brought to Tibet by the great Lama Atisha in the eleventh century. They became the heart practice of his followers, the renowned Kadampas, and remain today the essential meditations of all Mahayana yogis.

In this book, Lama Zopa Rinpoche explains one aspect of thought transformation, that of transforming problems into happiness. He uses as his basis the first section of Jigme Tenpe Nyima's text, as well as the *lojong* section of Pabongka Rinpoche's *Liberation in the Palm of Your Hand.*

Lama Zopa Rinpoche was born in 1946 in the Solu Khumbu region of Nepal and recognized at the age of three as the reincarnation of the Lawudo Lama, a great meditator from that area. Rinpoche became a monk and was educated in monasteries in Nepal and Tibet.

Rinpoche escaped to India in 1959 and continued his studies in the Tibetan refugee camp of Buxa Duar in northern India. Soon after this, he started receiving teachings from Lama Thubten Yeshe, remaining with him as his heart disciple.

Rinpoche himself began teaching in 1970, giving his first meditation course to Westerners at Kopan Monastery, which the lamas had founded near Boudhanath in the Kathmandu Valley. He and Lama Yeshe were invited to the West by their growing number of students and were soon traveling and teaching regularly around the world. The lamas remained together until Lama Yeshe passed away in March 1984.

Lama Zopa Rinpoche is now the spiritual head of the Foundation for the Preservation of the Mahayana Tradition (FPMT), the name given by Lama Yeshe to the Dharma centers and other activities set up by the lamas' students in Asia, Europe, America, Australia, and New Zealand. There are now more than one hundred such centers and projects. Rinpoche travels constantly between these centers, teaching and guiding his thousands of disciples. He is renowned as a perfect example of the teachings he gives, displaying all the qualities of a bodhisattva in his tireless and compassionate work for others.

Transforming Problems into Happiness is a revised edition of *Transforming Problems,* originally published in Nepal in 1988. Many people have contributed to the current edition, including Josh Bartok, Hermes Brandt, Don Brown, Ailsa Cameron, Merry Colony, Robina Courtin, Roy Fraser, David Kittelstrom, Roger Kunsang, Tim McNeill, Connie Miller, Kaye Miner, Nick Ribush, Ingeborg Sandberg, Sybil Schlesinger, Sarah Thresher, and Sally Walter. Special thanks to Tulku Thondup for his kind permission to reprint his translation of the root text.

Many people have already found *Transforming Problems* helpful in their lives. We hope that this revised edition will enable even more people to understand the source of their problems and to transform them into happiness.

Appendix: Root Text

Instructions on Turning Happiness and Suffering into the Path of Enlightenment

Jigme Tenpe Nyima
Translated by Tulku Thondup with Harold Talbott

*Homage to Arya Avalokiteshvara through the recollection
of his virtues, which are celebrated thus:*

He who is always happy because of the happiness of others,
and extremely distressed by the sufferings of others,
who has achieved the quality of great compassion—
he renounces caring about his own happiness and suffering.

I am going to write a brief instruction on accepting happiness and suffering as the path of enlightenment. It is the most priceless teaching in the world and a useful tool for a spiritual life.

THE WAY OF ACCEPTING SUFFERING AS THE PATH TO ENLIGHTENMENT

By Means of Relative Truth

Whenever affliction comes to you from beings or inanimate objects, if your mind gets used to perceiving only the suffering or the negative aspects, then even from a small negative incident, great mental pain will ensue. For it is in the nature of indulging in any concept, whether suffering or happiness, that the experience of this happiness or suffering will thereby be intensified. As this negative experience gradually becomes stronger, a time will come when most of what appears before you will become the cause of bringing you unhappiness, and happiness will never have a chance to arise. If you do not realize that the fault lies with your own mind's way of gaining experience, and if you blame external conditions alone, then the ceaseless flame of negative deeds such as hatred and suffering will increase. This is called: "All appearances arising in the form of enemies."

You should thoroughly understand that the reason living beings in the quarreling age are afflicted by suffering is fundamentally related to the weakness of their discriminative mind.

Thus, being invincible against obstacles, such as enemies, illnesses, and harmful spirits, does not mean that you can drive them away so that they will not recur. Rather, it means that they will not be able to arise as obstacles to the pursuit of the path of enlightenment. In order to succeed in using suffering as the support of the path, you should train yourself in the following two ways:

Reject the state of mind of exclusively desiring not to have suffering

Develop again and again the conviction that it is useless and harmful to feel anxiety and to dislike suffering by regarding it as totally unfavorable. Then, again and again with strong determination, think, "From now on, whatever suffering comes, I shall not be anxious," and gain experience of that.

1. The uselessness of considering suffering as something unfavorable

If you can remedy the suffering, then you don't need to be unhappy. If you cannot remedy it, then there is no benefit to being unhappy.

2. The great harm of considering suffering as something unfavorable

If you do not feel anxious, your strength of mind can help you to bear even great sufferings easily. They will feel light and insubstantial, like cotton. But anxiety will make even small sufferings intolerable.

For example, while you are thinking of a beautiful girl, even if you try to get rid of desire, you will only be burnt out. Similarly, if you concentrate on the painful characteristics of suffering, you will not be able to develop tolerance for it. So, as it is said in the "Instructions on Sealing the Doors of the Sense Faculties," your mind should not fasten on the negative characteristics of suffering; instead, you should gain experience in keeping your mind in its normal condition and remaining in its own state.

Developing the attitude of being happy that suffering arises

This is the practice of cultivating joy when suffering arises by regarding it as a support to the path of enlightenment. To apply this practice to your life, whenever suffering arises, you must have a training in a virtuous practice according to the ability of your mind. Otherwise, if, having merely a theoretical understanding, you think, "If I have certain skillful means to apply, the sufferings could bring this or that benefit," it will be difficult for you to achieve the goal. For, as it is said, "The goal is farther than the sky from the earth."

1. Suffering as the support of training in the mind of emergence from samsara

Think, "As long as I am wandering powerlessly in samsara, the arising of suffering is not an injustice, but is the nature of my being in samsara."

Develop revulsion toward samsara by thinking, "If it is difficult for me to bear even the little sufferings of the happy realms, then how can I bear the sufferings of the lower realms? Alas, samsara is an endless and bottomless ocean of suffering." With these thoughts, turn your mind to liberation.

2. Suffering as the support of training in taking refuge

Train in taking refuge by developing a strong belief and thinking, "The Three Precious Jewels are the only unbetraying refuges for those endangered by these kinds of fears throughout their succession of lives. From now on I will always depend on the refuges and will never renounce them in any circumstances!"

3. Suffering as the support of training in overcoming pride

Eliminate your pride and contempt for others, which are inimical to gaining any merit, by realizing, as discussed earlier, that you don't have any control over your own destiny and that you have not transcended the enslavement of suffering.

4. Suffering as the support for purification of unvirtuous deeds

Think carefully, "The sufferings I have experienced and other sufferings that are more unimaginably numerous and severe than those I have experienced are all solely the results of unvirtuous deeds." Think carefully about this with regard to the four following aspects:

The certainty of the process of karma
The tendency of karma to increase greatly
That you will not encounter the result of what you have not done
That the effects of what you have done will not be wasted

You should also think, "If I do not want suffering I should renounce the cause of suffering, which is unvirtuous deeds." In this way purify your previously accumulated unvirtuous deeds by means of the four powers and try to refrain from committing them again in the future.

5. Suffering as the support for attraction to virtue

Think long and carefully, "If I desire happiness, the opposite of suffering, I should try to practice its cause, which is virtue," and practice virtuous deeds through various means.

6. Suffering as the support for training in compassion

Think about other living things, who are also tortured by as much, if not more, pain as you are and train yourself by thinking, "How good it would be if they too became free from all sufferings!"

By this method of thinking, you will also understand the way of practicing loving-kindness, which is the intention to help those who are bereft of happiness.

7. Taking suffering as the support for the meditation that others are dearer than oneself

Think, "The reason I am not free from suffering is that I have been caring only about myself from beginningless time. Now I should practice caring only about others, the source of virtue and happiness."

Conclusion

It is very difficult to practice "taking suffering as the path of enlightenment" when you actually come face-to-face with difficult situations. So it is important to become familiar in advance with the trainings of virtue that are to be applied when unfavorable circumstances arise. Also, it makes a great difference if you apply a training in which you have clear experience.

Furthermore, it is not enough merely for suffering to become the support of virtuous training itself. You have to realize that the suffering has actually become the support of the path, and then you must feel a strong and stable stream of bliss, which is brought about by that realization.

For any of the foregoing categories of training you should think, "Just as the suffering I have undergone in the past has greatly helped me achieve happiness in many significant forms, the joy of high realms, and liberation from samsara, which are all difficult to obtain, so too the suffering I am now undergoing will also continue to help me to attain these same results. So, even if my suffering is severe, it is supremely agreeable. It is like a molasses desert mixed with cardamom and pepper." Think about this again and again and cultivate the experience of bliss of the mind.

By training in this way, the overwhelming nature or superabundance of mental bliss makes the sufferings of the sense faculties as if they were imperceptible. Thus, having a mind that cannot be hurt by suffering is the characteristic of those who overcome illness by tolerance. It should be noted that, according to this reasoning, this would also be the character-istic of those who overcome other obstacles as well, such as antagonists and evil spirits.

As mentioned above, the "reversing of the thought of dislike for suf-fering" is the foundation of "turning suffering into the path of enlight-enment" because, while your mind is disturbed and your courage is extinguished by anxiety, you will not be able to turn your suffering into the path.

Also, by training in the actual "taking suffering as the path of enlight-enment," you will improve the previous training, that is, the "reversing of the thought of dislike for suffering," because, as you actually experience an increase in virtues through suffering, you will grow increasingly coura-geous or cheerful.

It is said:

If you gradually train yourself through small sufferings, "by easy, gradual stages," as the saying goes, you will ultimately be able to train yourself in great sufferings also.

So, according to this instruction, you should train gradually, because it will be difficult for you to gain any experience beyond the scope of your present mental capacity.

In the intervals between meditation periods you should pray to the unexcelled Three Precious Jewels so that you will be able to turn suffering into the path. Then, when your mental strength has grown a little, make offerings to the Three Precious Jewels and spirits and implore them, saying: "In order that I may gain strength in the practice of virtuous trainings, please send me unfavorable circumstances." You should maintain the confidence of blissfulness and cheerfulness on all occasions.

When you are first learning this training it is important to keep mundane diversions at a distance. For amid such diversions you may become susceptible to the many negative influences of your companions' asking you, "How can you bear suffering and contempt?" The flurry of worries caused by adversaries, relatives, and wealth could defile and disturb your mind beyond control and cause bad habits. There are also various other distracting circumstances that could overpower your mind.

In solitary places, where these distractions are not present, the mind will be very clear. So it will be easy to concentrate on virtuous trainings.

For this reason, even the Chöd practitioners, when meditating on "stepping on or controlling suffering," at first avoid practicing near the harmful actions of men or amid worldly diversions. Instead, they train mainly with the apparitions of gods [positive spirits] and demons [negative spirits] in solitary cemeteries and power spots.

In brief, you should prevent attitudes of dislike toward internal illness, external antagonists, evil spirits, and unharmonious speech from arising, not only in order to make your mind impervious to misfortune and suffering, but also to bring bliss to your mind from the vicissitudes themselves. You should accustom yourself to generating only the feeling of liking them. To do this, you should cease to view harmful circumstances as negative and should make every effort to train yourself to view them as valuable, because whether things are pleasing or not depends on how your mind perceives them. For example, if a person is continuously aware of the faults in worldly pursuits, then, if his retinue and wealth increase, he will feel all the more revulsion toward them. On the other hand, if a person perceives worldly pursuits as beneficial, he will even aspire to increase his majestic power.

By practicing this kind of training, your mind will become gentle. Your attitude will become broad. You will become easy to be with. You will have a courageous mind. Your spiritual training will become free from obstacles. All bad circumstances will arise as glorious and auspicious. Your mind will always be satisfied by the joy of peace.

To practice the path of enlightenment in this quarreling age, you must never be without the armor of this kind of training. When you are not afflicted by the suffering of anxiety, not only will other sufferings disappear, like weapons dropping from the hands of soldiers, but in most cases, even the real negative forces, such as illnesses themselves, will automatically disappear. The Holy Ones of the past said:

> By not feeling any dislike toward or discontent about anything, your mind will remain undisturbed. When your mind is not disturbed, your energy will not be disturbed, and thereby other elements of the body will also not be disturbed. Because of this, your mind will not be disturbed, and so the wheel of joy will keep revolving.

They also said:

> As birds find it easy to injure horses and donkeys with sores on their backs, evil spirits or negative forces will easily find the opportunity to harm those whose nature is fearful. But it will be difficult to harm those whose nature is stable or strong.

Learned people realize that all happiness and suffering depend upon the mind and therefore seek happiness from the mind itself. They understand that, because the causes of happiness are complete within us, they are not dependent on external sources. With this realization, no matter what the afflictions, whether from beings or physical matter, they will not be able to hurt us. This same strength of mind shall also be with us at the time of death. We will always be free from the control of external afflictions.

The meditative absorption of bodhisattvas known as "overpowering of all elements by happiness" is also accomplished by this means.

Instead of seeking happiness within their minds, foolish people chase after external objects, hoping thereby to find happiness. But the pursuit of any worldly happiness, whether great or small, presents those people seeking it with many failures, such as their not being able to attain it, to associate with it, or to keep it in balance. For such foolish people, as a proverb says, "Control is in the hands of others as if their hair were tangled in a tree."

Enemies and robbers will find it easy to harm these foolish people. Even a little criticism will drive happiness away from their minds. Their happiness will never be reliable but will be as when a crow nurses a baby cuckoo: However much the crow nurtures the baby, it will be impossible for the baby cuckoo to become a baby crow. When such is the case, there will be nothing that is not tiresome for the gods [positive forces], miserable for demons [negative forces], and suffering for them [the foolish people].

This heart advice is the condensation of a hundred different crucial points in one. There are many other instructions, such as how to accept the hardship of asceticism for practicing the path, and how to turn illness and harmful effects into the path, as taught in *zhi che* teachings and so on. But here I have just written an easily understandable outline on accepting suffering as the support based on the teachings of Shantideva and his learned followers.

By Means of Absolute Truth

This is how to draw your mind to dwell contemplatively in supreme peace, the natural state of emptiness, in which unfavorable circumstances or even their names cannot be found, and how it is realized by means of reasoning-knowledge, such as the "refutation of the arising of phenomena from any of the four extremes."

Even when you are out of that contemplative state, you should overcome unfavorable circumstances by seeing them as being hollow, mere names, and as not arising in the manner that feelings of suffering arose in your mind when fear and intimidation occurred in the past.

THE WAY OF TAKING HAPPINESS AS THE PATH TO ENLIGHTENMENT

By Means of Relative Truth

If you slip under the control of happy circumstances or things that cause happiness, you will become proud, arrogant, and complacent, and this will obstruct your path toward enlightenment. But it is difficult not to fall under the sway of happiness, for, as Padampa says, "Men can bear great suffering, but only a little happiness."

Therefore, consider how all the various phenomena of happiness and their sources are impermanent and full of suffering. Make efforts to develop a strong revulsion toward them and to turn your mind away from careless behavior.

Again, you ought to think, "All the wealth and happiness of the world are insignificant and are linked with much harm." Nevertheless, some of it has value, as the Buddha says:

For a person whose freedom is impaired by suffering, it is very difficult to achieve enlightenment; but it will be easy for a person to achieve enlightenment if he is in comfort.

It is my great good fortune to have the opportunity to practice Dharma in happiness. Now I must buy Dharma with this happiness, and from the Dharma will happiness arise continuously. So I should train in making Dharma and happiness each other's support. Otherwise, like boiling water in a wooden pot, the final outcome will be the very same as what it was at the beginning." Thus you should achieve the essential goal of life by uniting whatever happiness and joy arises with Dharma. This is the view of Nagarjuna's *Precious Garland*.

If you are happy but do not recognize it, your happiness will not become the instrument of Dharma training, and you will be wasting your life with the hope of a separate happiness. Therefore, as the antidote to the hopes for having a separate happiness, you should apply appropriate methods among the trainings given above and should possess the ambrosia of contentment.

There are other ways to take happiness as the path, such as those based on the "instructions on training in bodhichitta" and on "remembering the kindness of the Three Precious Jewels." For the time being, however, this much is sufficient.

Further, in order to accept happiness as the path, as explained in the case of suffering, you should alternate the trainings of purification with the accumulation of merit in a solitary place.

By Means of Absolute Truth

You should understand it ("the way of accepting happiness as the path by means of absolute truth") by the training given earlier (that is, the training on suffering.)

CONCLUSION

If you cannot practice Dharma because of sorrow when you are suffering, and if you cannot practice Dharma because of your attachment to happiness when you are happy, then it will be impossible for you to have a chance to practice Dharma. So if you practice Dharma, there is nothing more essential than this training.

If you have this training, whatever kind of place you stay in, whether in a solitary place or a city; whatever the friends you associate with, whether good or bad; in whatever situation you find yourself, whether in riches or poverty, happiness or sorrow; whatever conversations you hear, whether praise or condemnation, good or bad, you will never be afraid that it might diminish you. Thus this training is called "the lion-like training."

Then whatever you do, your mind will be at ease and relaxed. Your attitude will be pure. Your final accomplishments will be excellent. Even though, physically, you are living in this impure land, your mind will be enjoying the glory of inconceivable bliss [peace] like the bodhisattvas of the pure lands. As the Kadampa lamas say:

By means of such training, happiness will be brought under control, and suffering will be ended. If you are alone, it will be the companion of sadness. If you are sick, it will nurse you.

Goldsmiths purify gold by melting it and make it flexible by rinsing it in water again and again. It is likewise with the mind: If, by taking happiness as the path, you develop ardent desire for the practice of the Dharma, and if, by taking suffering as the path, you cleanse your mind, then you shall easily attain the extraordinary meditative absorption that makes your mind and body capable of accomplishing what you wish.

I can see that this training is the most profound method for perfecting moral discipline, the root of the virtues. Because it generates non-attachment to happiness, the foundation of the extraordinary moral discipline of renunciation is established. Because it generates freedom from the fear of suffering, it makes the discipline pure. As it is said:

Giving is the basis of moral discipline. Patience is the cleanser of moral discipline.

By training this way now, when you reach the higher stages of the path your attainments will come about as it is said:

Bodhisattvas realize that all phenomena are like Maya
and they see that their births in samsara are like entering
   a joyful garden.
Therefore, either at the time of prosperity or decline,
they will not experience the danger of either emotional
   defilements or suffering.

Here are some illustrations from the life of the Buddha: Before attaining enlightenment, he renounced the universal rulership as if it were straw and sat by the Nairanjana River with no concern for the harshness of the austerities that he was practicing. This indicates that the development of equal taste of happiness and suffering was necessary for him to achieve the ambrosia (that is, full enlightenment).

After the Buddha attained enlightenment, on the one hand, the chiefs of human beings and gods up to the highest realms placed his feet on the crowns of their heads and offered him respect and service for all his needs and comfort. On the other hand, the Brahmin Bharadvaja abused him with a hundred allegations, a Brahmin's daughter slandered him with accusations of sexual misconduct, and he lived on rotten horse fodder for three months in the country of King Agnidatta, and so forth. Yet throughout all these the Buddha remained without any alternations of mind, excitement, or depression, just like Mount Sumeru, which cannot be moved by the wind. This indicates that it is necessary to develop equal taste of happiness and suffering in order to act for the benefit of living beings.

COLOPHON

It is appropriate for this teaching to be taught by those who are like the Lord Kadampas, who have a history of "not crying when there is suffering" and of having "great revulsion toward samsara when there is happiness." If a man like me teaches it, I am afraid that my own tongue will have contempt for me. But with my goal of achieving the habit of "equal taste" of the eight worldly affairs, I, the poor old man Tenpe Nyima, have written this in the Forest of Many Birds.

Glossary

Aggregates. The association of body and mind; a person comprises five aggregates: form, feeling, recognition, consciousness, and compositional factors.

Atisha (982–1054). The renowned Indian Buddhist master who came to Tibet to help in the revival of Buddhism and who established the Kadam tradition. His text, *Lamp of the Path to Enlightenment*, is the basis of the *lamrim*.

Bodhichitta. The altruistic aspiration to achieve enlightenment in order to enlighten all living beings.

Bodhisattva. One who possesses bodhichitta.

Buddha. A fully awakened, or enlightened, being. *See* enlightenment.

Buddhadharma. *See* Dharma.

Buddha-potential. Refers to the emptiness, or ultimate nature, of the mind. Because of this nature, every sentient being possesses the potential to become fully enlightened, a Buddha.

Cyclic existence. *See* samsara.

Delusions. The thoughts that are the cause of suffering. The three root delusions are ignorance, anger, and attachment.

Dharma. The teachings of the Buddha.

Disturbing thoughts. *See* delusions.

Eight freedoms. The eight states from which a perfect human rebirth is free:

(1) being born in a hell realm; (2) being born as a hungry ghost; (3) being born as an animal; (4) being born as a barbarian; (5) being born as a long-life god; (6) holding wrong views; (7) being born in a dark age when no Buddha has descended; (8) being born with defective mental or physical faculties.

Eight worldly dharmas. The worldly concerns that generally motivate the actions of ordinary beings: (1) being happy when acquiring something; (2) being unhappy when not acquiring something; (3) wanting to be happy; (4) not wanting to be unhappy; (5) wanting to hear interesting sounds; (6) not wanting to hear uninteresting sounds; (7) wanting praise; (8) not wanting criticism.

Emptiness. The absence or lack of true existence. Ultimately, every phenomenon is empty of existing truly, or from its own side, or independently. *See* merely labeled.

Enlightenment. Full awakening; buddhahood; omniscience; the ultimate goal of Mahayana Buddhist practice, attained when all limitations have been removed from the mind and all positive potential has been realized; a state characterized by unlimited compassion, skill, and wisdom.

Evil-gone realms. *See* lower realms.

Five degenerations. The degenerations of life span, view, disturbing thoughts, sentient beings, and time.

Five powers. The five are: (1) the power of determination: the force of setting a positive motivation; (2) the power of familiarity: training constantly in the thought of bodhichitta; (3) the power of the white seed: increasing the force of bodhichitta; (4) the power of putting the blame: repudiating self-cherishing, the source of all problems; and (5) the power of aspiration: dedicating one's merit toward the development of bodhichitta.

Four noble truths. The subject of the Buddha's first discourse: true suffering, true cause of suffering, true cessation of suffering, and true path to the cessation of suffering.

Four opponent powers. When purifying negative karma, one applies these four: (1) the power of the basis; (2) the power of regret; (3) the power of the remedy; and (4) the power of making the determination never to commit the action again.

Geshe. Literally, "virtuous spiritual friend" and a term given to the great Kadampas; now, the doctoral title conferred upon those who have completed extensive studies and examinations at Gelug monastic universities.

Graduated path to enlightenment. Originally outlined in Tibet by Atisha in *Lamp of the Path to Enlightenment,* the graduated path is a step-by-step presentation of the Buddha's teachings.

Guru Puja. Text of an extensive practice that involves making prayers, requests, and offerings to the lama.

Imprints. The seeds, or potentials, left on the mind by karma, positive or negative actions of body, speech, and mind.

Kadampa geshe. A practitioner of the Buddhist tradition that originated in Tibet in the eleventh century with the teachings of Atisha; Kadampa geshes are renowned for their practice of thought transformation.

Karma. The law of cause and effect; the process whereby virtuous actions of body, speech, and mind lead to happiness and nonvirtuous ones to suffering.

Kopan. The monastery founded in 1970 by Lama Yeshe and Lama Zopa Rinpoche near Boudhanath, in the Kathmandu Valley of Nepal.

Lama. The Tibetan word for guru; literally, "heavy," as in heavy with Dharma knowledge.

Lama Tsongkhapa (1357–1419). The revered teacher and practitioner who founded the Gelug school of Tibetan Buddhism and who was a manifestation of Manjushri, the buddha of wisdom.

Lawudo Cave. The cave in the Solu Khumbu region of Nepal where the Lawudo Lama lived and meditated for many years. Lama Zopa Rinpoche is recognized as the reincarnation of the Lawudo Lama.

Liberation. The state of complete liberation from samsara; nirvana.

Lower realms. The three realms of cyclic existence with the greatest suffering: hell realm, realm of the hungry ghosts, and animal realm. *See* samsara.

Mahayana. The Great Vehicle; the path of the bodhisattvas, those seeking enlightenment in order to enlighten all other sentient beings.

Mandala. The symbolic offering to the Buddha of the entire purified universe.

Marpa (1012–1099). A great Tibetan Buddhist translator; a founding figure of the Kagyu order and the root guru of Milarepa.

Merely labeled. Every phenomenon exists relatively as a mere label, merely imputed by the mind. *See* emptiness.

Merit. The positive energy accumulated in the mind as a result of virtuous actions of body, speech, and mind.

Migratory beings. Another term for sentient beings, who migrate from rebirth to rebirth within the six realms of samsara.

Milarepa (1040–1123). The great ascetic yogi and poet who attained enlightenment in one lifetime; a founding figure of the Kagyu order.

Nagarjuna. The great Indian scholar who lived approximately six hundred years after Buddha's death; propounder of the Middle Way, who clarified the ultimate meaning of the Buddha's teachings on emptiness.

Nyingma. The oldest of the four orders of Tibetan Buddhism; the others are Sakya, Kagyu, and Gelug.

Omniscient mind. *See* enlightenment.

Pervasive compounding suffering. The most subtle of the three types of suffering, it refers to the nature of the five aggregates, contaminated by karma and delusion.

Precious human body. The rare human state, qualified by the eight freedoms and the ten richnesses, which is the ideal condition for practicing Dharma and attaining enlightenment.

Purification. The removal, or cleansing, of negative karma and its imprints from the mind.

Refuge. Reliance upon Buddha, Dharma, and Sangha for guidance on the path to enlightenment.

Renunciation. The state of mind of not having the slightest attraction to samsaric perfections for even a second.

Samsara. Cyclic existence; the six realms: the lower realms of the hell beings, hungry ghosts, and animals, and the upper realms of the humans, demi-gods, and gods; the recurring cycle of death and rebirth within one or another of the six realms; also refers to the contaminated aggregates of a sentient being.

Sangha. The third object of refuge; absolute Sangha are those who have directly realized emptiness; relative Sangha are ordained monks and nuns.

Sentient being. Any living being within the six samsaric realms who has not yet reached enlightenment.

Shantideva (685–763). The great Indian scholar and bodhisattva who wrote the *Bodhicharyavatara (Guide to the Bodhisattva's Way of Life),* one of the essential Mahayana texts.

Suffering of change. What is normally regarded as pleasure, which, because of its transitory nature, sooner or later turns into suffering.

Suffering of suffering. The commonly recognized experiences of pain, discomfort, and unhappiness.

Sutra. The exoteric discourses of the Buddha; a scriptural text and the teachings and practices it contains.

Tantra. The esoteric teachings of the Buddha; a scriptural text and the teachings and practices it contains.

Ten richnesses. The ten qualities that characterize a perfect human rebirth: (1) being born as a human being; (2) being born in a Dharma country; (3) being born with sound mental and physical faculties; (4) being free of the five extreme actions; (5) having faith in the Buddha's teachings; (6) being born when a Buddha has descended, (7) when the teachings have been revealed, (8) when the teachings are still alive, (9) when there are still followers of the teachings; and (10) having the necessary conditions to practice Dharma.

Three Jewels. *See* Triple Gem.

Three levels of vows. The pratimoksha vows, or vows of individual liberation, the bodhisattva vows, and the tantric vows.

Tonglen (taking and giving). The Mahayana meditation technique of taking upon oneself all the sufferings and causes of sufferings of all sentient beings and of giving to others all one's own merit, possessions, and happiness.

Triple Gem. Buddha, Dharma, and Sangha.

True cause of suffering. The second of the four noble truths, it refers to karma and delusion.

True cessation of suffering. The third of the four noble truths, it is the state of liberation from suffering and the true causes of suffering.

True existence. The type of existence that everything appears to possess; in fact, everything is empty of true existence.

True path. The fourth noble truth, it refers to the methods of Dharma practice that lead sentient beings to the true cessation of suffering.

True suffering. The first of the four noble truths, it refers to the fact that all con- ditioned existence is pervaded by suffering.

Yogi. A disciplined meditator.

Suggested Further Reading

Chödrön, Pema. *Start Where You Are: A Guide to Compassionate Living*. Boston: Shambhala Publications, 1994.

Chodron, Thubten. *Open Heart, Clear Mind*. Ithaca: Snow Lion Publications, 1991.

Dharmaraksita. *The Wheel of Sharp Weapons*. Trans. Geshe Dhargyey et al. Dharamsala: Library of Tibetan Works and Archives, 1976.

Dilgo Khyentse Rinpoche. *Enlightened Courage: An Explanation of Atisha's Seven Point Mind Training*. Ithaca: Snow Lion Publications, 1993.

Gomo Tulku. *Becoming a Child of the Buddhas: A Simple Clarification of the Root Verses of Seven-Point Mind Training*. Boston: Wisdom Publications, 1997.

Gyatso, Tenzin, the Fourteenth Dalai Lama. *Freedom in Exile: The Autobiography of the Dalai Lama*. San Francisco: Harper San Francisco, 1991.

——— et al. *Four Essential Buddhist Commentaries*. Dharamsala: Library of Tibetan Works and Archives, 1982.

———. *The Meaning of Life: Buddhist Perspectives on Cause and Effect*. Trans. and ed. Jeffrey Hopkins. Boston: Wisdom Publications, 2000.

———. *MindScience: An East-West Dialogue*. Eds. Daniel Goleman and Robert A. F. Thurman. Boston: Wisdom Publications, 1991.

———. *Opening the Eye of New Awareness*. Trans. Donald S. Lopez. Boston: Wisdom Publications, 1999.

————. *Sleeping, Dreaming, and Dying: An Exploration of Consciousness with the Dalai Lama*. Ed. Francisco Varela. Boston: Wisdom Publications, 1997.

Gyeltsen, Geshe Tsultrim. *Compassion: The Key to Great Awakening*. Boston: Wisdom Publications, 1997.

Hopkins, Jeffrey. *The Tantric Distinction: A Buddhist's Reflections on Compassion and Emptiness*. Boston: Wisdom Publications, 1999.

Khunu Rinpoche. *Vast as the Heaven, Deep as the Sea: Verses in Praise of Bodhicitta*. Boston: Wisdom Publications, 1999.

Kongtrul, Jamgon. *The Great Path of Awakening*. Trans. Ken McLeod. Boston: Shambhala Publications, 1988.

Landaw, Jonathan and Janet Brooke. *Prince Siddhartha: The Story of Buddha*. Boston: Wisdom Publications, 1984.

Levey, Joel and Michelle. *The Fine Arts of Relaxation, Concentration and Meditation*. Boston: Wisdom Publications, 1991.

McDonald, Kathleen. *How to Meditate*. Boston: Wisdom Publications, 1984.

Nagarjuna. *The Precious Garland*. Trans. Jeffrey Hopkins and Lati Rinpoche. In *The Buddhism of Tibet*. Ithaca: Snow Lion Publications, 1987.

Pabongka Rinpoche. *Liberation in the Palm of Your Hand*. Trans. Michael Richards. Boston: Wisdom Publications, 1991.

Pän-ch'en Lo-zang Ch'ö-kyi Gyäl-tsän. *The Guru Puja*. Trans. Alex Berzin et al. Dharamsala: Library of Tibetan Works and Archives, 1981.

Rabten, Geshe. *The Essential Nectar*. Trans. Martin Willson. Boston: Wisdom Publications, 1984.

———— and Geshe Ngawang Dhargyey. *Advice from a Spiritual Friend*. Trans. and ed. Brian Beresford. Boston: Wisdom Publications, 2001.

Shantideva. *A Guide to the Bodhisattva's Way of Life*. Trans. Stephen Batchelor. Dharamsala: Library of Tibetan Works and Archives, 1979.

————. *Way of the Bodhisattva: Translation of the Bodhicharyavatara*. Trans. Padmakara Translation Group. Boston: Shambhala Publications, 1997.

Sopa, Geshe Lhundub. *Peacock in a Poison Grove: Two Tibetan Mind Training Texts.* Ed. Michael Sweet and Leonard Zwilling. Boston: Wisdom Publications, 2001.

Thondup Rinpoche, Tulku (trans.). *Enlightened Living: Teachings of Tibetan Buddhist Masters.* Ed. Harold Talbott. Kathmandu: Rangjung Yeshe Publications, 1997.

Trungpa, Chogyam. *Training the Mind & Cultivating Loving-Kindness.* Ed. Judith L. Lief. Boston: Shambhala Publications, 1993.

gTsan-smyon Heruka. *The Life of Milarepa.* Trans. Lobsang Lhalungpa. London: Granada, 1979.

Tsongkapa. *The Principal Teachings of Buddhism.* Classics of Middle Asia. Trans. Geshe Lobsang Tharchin with Michael Roach. New Jersey: Mahayana Sutra and Tantra Press, 1988.

Wallace, B. Alan. *A Passage from Solitude: Training the Mind in a Life Embracing the World: A Modern Commentary on Tibetan Buddhist Mind Training.* Ithaca: Snow Lion Publications, 1992.

Wangchen, Geshe Namgyal. *Awakening the Mind: Basic Buddhist Meditations.* Boston: Wisdom Publications, 1995.

Wangyal, Geshe. *The Door of Liberation.* Boston: Wisdom Publications, 1995.

Yeshe, Lama Thubten. *Introduction to Tantra: A Vision of Totality.* Ed. Jonathan Landaw. Boston: Wisdom Publications, 1987.

———— and Lama Zopa Rinpoche. *Wisdom Energy.* Ed. Jonathan Landaw with Alexander Berzin. Boston: Wisdom Publications, 2000.

Zopa Rinpoche, Lama. *The Door to Satisfaction: The Heart Advice of a Tibetan Buddhist Master.* Boston: Wisdom Publications, 1993.

Also by Lama Zopa Rinpoche

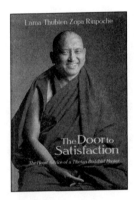

THE DOOR TO SATISFACTION
The Heart Advice
of a Tibetan Buddhist Master

Lama Zopa Rinpoche

Lama Zopa reveals the essential meaning of an ancient thought-training text that he discovered in his retreat cave high in the Himalayas of Nepal. The message is simple: you can stop all problems forever and gain perfect peace of mind by practicing the thought-training methods explained herein. At the beginning of this teaching, he startled his audience when he declared, "Only when I read this text did I come to know what the practice of Buddhism really means!" Open this book and open the door to a timeless path leading to wisdom and joy.

"His is truly a path with heart." —*NAPRA ReView*

184 pages, 0-86171-058-4, $12.50

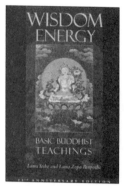

WISDOM ENERGY
Basic Buddhist Teachings

Lama Yeshe and Lama Zopa Rinpoche

"In this wonderful book, two highly accomplished Tibetan Buddhist teachers demonstrate their remarkable talent for illuminating sometimes complex ideas in a way that is easily graspable by Westerners. This lucid introduction to Buddhism is directly relevant to modern life. I highly recommend it."
—Howard C. Cutler, M.D., co-author of *The Art of Happiness*

160 pages, 0-86171-170-X, $14.95

Available in Fall 2001

ULTIMATE HEALING
The Power of Compassion

Lama Zopa Rinpoche

We experience illness on a physical level, but in order to be healed, we must understand where true healing begins: within our own minds. *Ultimate Healing* shows us that by transforming our minds, especially through developing compassion, we can eliminate the ultimate cause of all disease.

In addition to relating stories of people who have recovered from disease through meditation, Lama Zopa presents practical healing meditations, including white-light healing, compassion meditation, "taking and giving," and techniques to cure depression. *Ultimate Healing* shows that by opening up to the truths of impermanence, interdependence, and the suffering of others, we can heal our bodies, our lives, and the world around us.

288 pages, 0-86171-195-5, $16.95

The Foundation for the Preservation
of the Mahayana Tradition

The Foundation for the Preservation of the Mahayana Tradition (FPMT) is an international network of Buddhist centers and activities dedicated to the transmission of Mahayana Buddhism as a practiced and living tradition. The FPMT was founded in 1975 by Lama Thubten Yeshe and is now under the spiritual direction of Lama Thubten Zopa Rinpoche. It is composed of Dharma teaching centers, monasteries, retreat centers, publishing houses, healing centers, hospices, and projects for the construction of stupas, statues, and other holy objects.

To receive a listing of these centers and projects as well as news about the activities throughout this global network, please contact:

FPMT International Office
125B La Posta Rd, Taos NM 87571 USA
Tel: (505) 758-7766 • Fax: (505) 758-7765
Email: fpmt@compuserve.com • www.fpmt.org

The Lama Yeshe Wisdom Archive

The Lama Yeshe Wisdom Archive (LYWA) is the collected works of Lama Thubten Yeshe and Lama Thubten Zopa Rinpoche. The Archive was founded in 1996 by Lama Zopa Rinpoche, its spiritual director, to make available in various ways the teachings it contains.

The Lama Yeshe Wisdom Archive
PO Box 356, Weston MA 02493 USA
Tel: (781) 899-9587   Fax: (781) 899-7183
www.lamayeshe.com

Wisdom Publications

Wisdom Publications, a not-for-profit publisher, is dedicated to making authentic Buddhist works available for the benefit of all. We publish translations of the sutras and tantras, commentaries and teachings of past and contemporary Buddhist masters, and original works by the world's leading Buddhist scholars. We publish our titles with the appreciation of Buddhism as a living philosophy and with the special commitment to preserve and transmit important works from all the major Buddhist traditions.

If you would like more information or a copy of our mail order catalogue, please write to us at:

Wisdom Publications
199 Elm Street, Somerville, Massachusetts 02144 USA
Telephone: (617) 776-7416 • Fax: (617) 776-7841
E-mail: sales@wisdompubs.org
Web Site: http://www.wisdompubs.org

The Wisdom Trust

As a not-for-profit publisher, Wisdom Publications is dedicated to the publication of fine Dharma books for the benefit of all sentient beings and dependent upon the kindness and generosity of sponsors in order to do so. If you would like to make a donation to Wisdom, please contact our Somerville office.

Thank you.

Wisdom Publications is a non-profit, charitable 501(c)(3) organization affiliated with the Foundation for the Preservation of the Mahayana Tradition (FPMT).